The Man Behind
the Curtain
a memoir

Jessica Renee

with
Valerie Dimino

Possibilities Press

Cover design by Clarissa Kezen of CK Book Cover Designs
Interior layout by Amber Helt of Rooted in Writing

Publisher's Cataloging-in-Publication Data

Names: Renee, Jessica, author. | Dimino, Valerie, author.
Title: The man behind the curtain : a memoir / Jessica Renee ; with Valerie Dimino.
Description: [Lakeville, New York] : Possibilities Press, [2022]
Identifiers: ISBN: 979-8-9859400-0-8 (hardcover) | 979-8-9859400-1-5 (paperback) | 979-8-9859400-2-2 (e-book)
Subjects: LCSH: Renee, Jessica. | Adult child sexual abuse victims—United States—Biography. | Sexually abused teenagers—United States—Biography. | Rape—United States. | Incest—United States. | Child sexual abuse—United States. | Sexual harassment—United States. | Blaming the victim—United States. | Blame—Social aspects—United States. | Mothers and daughters—United States. | Husbands and wives—United States—Religious aspects—Southern Baptist Convention. | Marriage—Religious aspects—Southern Baptist Convention. | Women in the Southern Baptist Convention—Social aspects. | Girls—Crimes against—Social aspects. | Liability for child sexual abuse—United States. | Trials (Child sexual abuse)—United States. | Child molesters—Social aspects—United States. | Rapists—Social aspects—United States. | Sexual abuse victims' writings, American. | LCGFT: True crime stories. | Autobiographies. | BISAC: TRUE CRIME / Sexual Assault. | SOCIAL SCIENCE / Sexual Abuse & Harassment. | BIOGRAPHY & AUTOBIOGRAPHY / Personal Memoirs.
Classification: LCC: HV6570.7 .R46 2022 | DDC: 362.76/40973—dc23

www.valeriedimino.com

For all the other warriors,
with stories told, untold,
or soon to be told

For Nana and Poppy

For Bella,
loyal companion

Contents

Preface   vii

Prologue   1
What I Remember   4
Ghost Stories   19
Caught in the Act   33
Speaking My Truth   44
Watching Others Speak   68
A Black Hole   79
A Rescue   93
Devil Be Gone   109
New Girl in an Old Town   130
A Victim on Trial   155
A Church Against a Child   183
No Child Deserves to Live in Fear   196
Banishing the Ghosts   209

Afterword   213
Acknowledgments   229
About the Authors   235

Preface

by coauthor Valerie Dimino

This is the true story of Jessica Renee and her family, who have been estranged because of the criminal actions of her stepfather, Mitch. Though Jessica had some opportunity to speak out as the criminal case against Mitch unfolded, her words were often limited, interrupted, questioned, and twisted. They were made into tools in a complicated, unfair game. She was forced to reveal her story, many times over, on other people's terms, often only to be met with further suffering. For years since, she has longed to take ownership of the narrative, knowing she has more to tell—and she hopes that sharing her story in this way might help others to find courage and comfort in surviving their own journeys.

Through interviews, emails, and court transcripts, I have immersed myself in the details of Jessica's story in an effort to help her speak, to write the words on her behalf. We have worked in close collaboration throughout this project to ensure that I represent the events and her perspective accurately.

There are many sides to every story, of course, but these are facts:

1. When detectives came to Mitch Wilson's door and asked to speak to Jessica, he did not ask why or what was wrong; he merely pointed in the direction of her bedroom door.
2. When the detectives interviewed Mitch at the police station later that night, he slid his car keys across the table and described to them where he'd parked. The detectives told me they interpreted this to mean that Mitch knew he was not going home.
3. When the detectives asked Mitch that night whether Jessica's accusations against him were true, his response was, "If she says it's true, then that's what it is. It is what it is."
4. After four years of criminal investigation and court hearings, Mitch was convicted on thirteen counts and sentenced to eight years in prison. He will be registered as a violent sex offender for the rest of his life.
5. Jessica's mother maintained her relationship with Mitch, sat with the defense team throughout the court hearings, and reduced contact with her daughter to the point that, to this day, they have no relationship.

These facts form the foundation upon which the rest of Jessica's story stands. While others may remember—or choose to portray—certain details differently, what follows is her account of those pivotal years and how they challenged her, shaped her, and ultimately strengthened her.

Jessica's perspective is corroborated by several experts far too familiar with stories like this—the detectives who worked on her case, her lawyer, her counselor—all of whom you'll hear from later in this book. But first we need to experience this through Jessica's eyes.

Some names and identifying details of people and places have been changed, including when they appear in excerpts from court transcripts or recorded interviews.

While the words are mine—shaped by all that Jessica and others have so generously shared with me—the experiences, battle scars, and devastating strength that helped to form the words are hers, carried silently for years.

It has been an honor to help her find her voice.

Prologue

I SPENT MUCH OF MY ADOLESCENCE KEEPING QUIET.
During the years that my stepfather, Mitch, was abusing me,
fear and shame drew a thick cloak over any words I might
have been tempted to say about it. The investigation and trial
that followed often forced me to speak in ways I wasn't ready
to, yet at the same time they enveloped me in a silence that
was deeper and darker still, a numbed half existence that left
me skeptical of everyone around me, questioning even my
own identity. Those years stretched on almost as long as the
abuse itself had, a continuation of it in many ways, coated
with a new kind of torment. The tension with my family and
the repercussions that the truth would have on our future
loomed too large to ignore, often chasing away my words and
making me regret the ones I had allowed. There were long
silences that thrummed in my ears, unspoken shouts that
echoed in my mind.

But I'm tired of being silenced. For the sake of my own
story and others like mine, I'm ready to speak now.

There's no way for me to know what Mitch or anyone

else involved in this story was thinking or what drove their actions. I only know how their actions affected me and altered the course of my life. What I present here are my memories and perceptions, meticulously reexamined and verified to the best of my ability, including by the professionals who worked on my case. I'm well aware that others may want to try to contradict me and—again and again, still—to silence me. But this is *my* story. And I stand firmly behind its truth.

Sharing this at twenty-four years old, I have the advantage of analyzing these formative, traumatic experiences from some distance, now that I'm safely on the other side of them. But that shaken eleven-year-old girl is still rooted inside of me, not just as a piece of my past but as a perspective I still draw from all too readily at times. I don't ever want to forget that version of myself, and I feel like I owe her a lot. But I'm working on growing far beyond that piece of me, using it to fuel great things. It has not been an easy path.

As I work hard at carving out a life on my own terms, I'm aware every day of all that Mitch took from me and all that I'm still working to overcome. My mom and brother no longer speak to me, and many of my friends have turned away too. I dropped out of college due to the stress and time commitment of seemingly endless court dates. I've had to cross paths with friends of my estranged family everywhere from the grocery store to my counselor's waiting room, and I even worked with some of them for a few years, making for some painful office banter. Mitch robbed me of the comfort I should be able to find in friendships and especially romantic relationships. Self-confidence, work ethic, and even just the motivation to get out of bed in the morning sometimes feel out of reach. I see so many people my age believing that the wide world awaits them with infinite, carefree possibilities, and I ache to find that kind of hope for myself.

For the crimes he committed against me, Mitch is serving eight years in prison and is quickly approaching his release date. Meanwhile, I feel I've been given a life sentence. I will carry this guilt, this regret, and this fear with me always.

I will forever be someone who was raped and sexually assaulted. I can't erase that part of my story, despite how much I've wished I could. What I've just recently started to accept, though, is that those experiences do not need to define me. I will not *let* them define me. I've struggled in silence for too long, assuming others wouldn't understand and would judge me. I've told myself that my voice doesn't need to be heard—or, worse, that it doesn't deserve to be. But I see now that I've been letting myself be punished for someone else's crimes. Maybe I can change what this part of my story means. Maybe it can be a source of power more than pain.

Along the landmine-ridden road to Mitch's imprisonment, I lost not only my stepfather but my mother and brother, who both chose him over me. I lost my role as daughter and sister. I was dragged into the role of victim the first time Mitch put his hands on me; I found the courage to speak from that role only years later, and I am still trying to process how thoroughly that role came to define me and my surroundings. *Victim* came to mean *outcast, interrogated, alone*. I am trying now to make it mean more, to take pride in its synonymy with *survivor*, to make it mean something like *warrior*.

What I Remember

I THINK MY MOTHER KNEW THAT HER HUSBAND WAS raping me. Maybe she didn't know the full extent of it—that he would treat me like his wife when she was away, sleeping side by side in their bed all night, waking up with my underwear damp and sticky—but she must have known something was wrong. She had nearly walked in on us several times; didn't she wonder why he'd run out so quickly?

She had even asked me about it, more than once. She had asked me outright if Mitch had touched me, if he had done anything inappropriate to me. She would slip the question in casually while we were busy with something else, like cleaning my room together, our hands and eyes occupied with other, more tangible things.

My answer: "Not really."

Then the conversation would taper away.

Should I have given a more straightforward answer? Should she have understood that anything other than an unequivocal "no" should be cause enough for concern? Absolutely—but this was the cycle we were caught in; day after day of avoidance, denial, and further sexual advances from my stepfather. It was like each one of us was maintaining a charade—that things were normal, that we were okay—and wondering which misstep, which unconvincing line, might make it all crumble.

When the abuse started, I was only eleven, so I'm not sure I *could* have answered my mother's questions more honestly. I was a child. There were pink and orange polka dots covering my bedroom walls, a fuzzy pink chair I'd curl up in with a book, a basket of Barbies in the corner. Sex was not in my vocabulary. I wouldn't have known how to describe what Mitch was doing or why it made me feel so strange. I'd see a classmate's dad hug her for a long time and think, *Maybe they have the same kind of relationship we do.* Mitch would show me naked women in pornographic magazines and tell me, "This is what I like." I just thought the women were models. He would unlock the bathroom door with a bobby pin and come in while I was showering, open the curtain, and ask me some casual question, like what I wanted for dinner. These things happened so routinely and matter-of-factly that I had no baseline for what was normal.

Some patterns which later became more disturbing were, early on, too easily mistaken for positive affection: comforting me when I was scared, or encouraging me to come to him if I wanted permission to do something, like go to a homecoming dance or have a Myspace account, that I thought my mom would say no to. He would offer to talk to Mom about it for me—my advocate, my influencer on the inside. I felt like Mitch loved me and had my back; he enjoyed spending time with me. Those can be alluring things for a kid, especially when coming from someone filling the role of the formerly absent father figure.

The word *stepfather* sometimes conveys a level of separation: someone less well-known, less close, a new figure being introduced into a life and bringing change along with him. But I don't remember life before Mitch. I was about three years old when he and my mom got together. Mom was only seventeen when she had me, and my biological dad was never really involved. The last time my parents spoke was when my dad signed over full custody, when I was just a little over a year old. Mitch was the only father I knew. I called him Dad. Throughout the years of abuse, it kept coming back to that for me: even if I suspected—or, later, knew—he had crossed a line, even if I felt uncomfortable or dirty or scared, he was still my dad. It was like he was two different people; I could separate the person from the behavior. I had to.

In many ways, I was closer to Mitch than to my mom. He was the one who helped my little brother, Caleb, and me with our homework, played games with us, cooked us dinner. I felt comfortable talking to him. If I needed advice or had to ask a favor, I would always go to Mitch; my mom was too likely to get upset.

She got upset easily. Once, Caleb and I made cheeseburgers for dinner while Mom was out, to surprise her when she got home. Her only reaction was to yell at us because we'd gotten oil on the stove she'd cleaned that morning. She yelled at Mitch, too, for having helped us, for letting us make a mess.

I remember thinking then, as a ten-year-old, *All we have to do is wipe it off.* But I didn't dare say that. Maybe cleaning a kitchen was more complicated than I knew. Maybe we should have known not to try to cook. Maybe I was the one who was wrong.

So many of my memories are divisive like that: Mitch, Caleb, and me playing UNO around the table for Wednesday-night game night while Mom sat on the couch and watched TV. Telling a joke that dissolved the three of us into giggles while Mom's face stayed still and silent.

I don't have many memories of us all together as a family —nothing that stands out like the sentimental home-movie moments that play back in slow motion on TV shows. We took a vacation to Myrtle Beach one summer. The most vivid memory I have from it is getting swimmer's ear. And we went to church together, of course, as so many Tennessean families did. The Southern Baptist community there was so large and intertwined, it was like its own village. Most of my friends went to the same church I did. Even if we went to different schools, I'd get to see them several times a week, between Sunday service, youth group, and extra meetings and activities. Church was not only about religion in the traditional sense but a seemingly sacred coming together, a communion of community, a combination social hour and nourishing of the soul.

Most of my weekends and summers were spent with my maternal grandparents, Nana and Poppy. Caleb rarely joined me there; he spent a lot of time with Mitch's parents. It's weird, now, to add it up and think about how often we both were away from home. It was just the norm. It makes me think my mom must not really have cared about spending time with us. It often felt like Mitch was the only one of us she loved. And Caleb had better odds than me, since he was half Mitch. I was an outlier.

I remember my mom always being very serious. And often screaming. I don't have any silly, playful memories of her. Her sense of humor amounted to a sarcasm so thick that, on the rare occasion she would make a joke, I would think she was being serious and unnervingly mean. I never felt like she had my back. I couldn't confide in her, couldn't talk to her about boys or drama with my friends, couldn't ask her about the changes my body was going through or the hormonal emotional gymnastics that came along with that. She would get upset if I even hugged a boy; how could I confide in her about crushes or ask her about sex? Her attitude toward me was so different from one day to the next. She could be loving, sometimes, but there seemed to be no pattern or logic behind it, much as I looked for one. If I woke up to the smell of pancakes, I knew it was going to be a good day. But I was always wondering, always waiting for those signals of safety.

My alliance with Mitch in those earlier years was a big part of what made it so confusing when he started to abuse me. He used our closeness to his advantage; the trust and comfort level he had established served as a foundation for the abuse that followed. Even now, more than a decade later, it hurts to wonder how much of that bond he fostered when I was younger was just a matter of softening me up in preparation to abuse me more easily.

It's so frustrating when people oversimplify abusive situations by asking if the victims tried to resist. Often, resisting does nothing or only makes the situation worse. I had tried to say no to Mitch's advances many times in the beginning. But he brandished his power over me expertly. He had built up my trust in him—helping me get out of being grounded by Mom, getting my cell phone back for me after she'd taken it away as a punishment, giving me the okay to go to a school dance. I would later come to see all of those behaviors as carefully calculated; he needed my trust so that he could later wield it against me.

But I remember that even the closeness I felt with Mitch in the earlier days, before the abuse started, had an aura of caution surrounding it. Maybe it came partially from knowing my biological father hadn't stuck around, and maybe partially from the strangeness I felt about being adopted by

Mitch. I remember I had wanted to say no to the adoption, and that Nana had had a bad feeling about it too—she always had more of a mother's intuition than my mom did. But it wasn't something they were offering up for consideration; it was simply set into motion, and I was swept along in the tidal wave. My mom made a spectacle of it, throwing a pizza party for my sixth-grade class to celebrate—calling more attention to the already-awkward change in my last name and inviting a lot of questions from classmates at an age when scrutiny is desperately avoided. Even then, I felt the commotion Mom was stirring up about it wasn't for me, but for her. She had solidified something; she was putting this polished new status on the trophy shelf. Now, I see her enthusiasm as affected, scripted. She was forcing overly sweetened frosting on me by heaping spoonfuls. It's left a sickening aftertaste, even all these years later.

Now we were really a family. Now we were complete. Now the Daddy role was filled and formalized.

We had moved from my small-town childhood home in Western New York to Tennessee that summer, the year I turned eleven—allegedly because the manufacturing company Mitch worked for was closing its New York location and relocating his job, but that closure never happened. In hindsight, my grandparents and I believe he was grooming the situation, a classic pedophile tactic to make their victims vulnerable and easier to manipulate; I wouldn't know anyone in Tennessee, wouldn't have any friends to turn to and confide in. Mitch was physically removing me from my safety net, from any sense of familiarity or security.

The timing seemed no coincidence either. Nana had found out that Mitch had been pulling my pants and panties down and spanking my bare butt when I was in trouble, at ten and eleven years old. When she confronted Mom about how inappropriate that was, Mom yelled at her to get out of her house. We weren't allowed to see Nana and Poppy for several months, so they sued for visitation rights, to try to protect both Caleb and me. That reinstating of my grandparents' role in my life seems to have been the immediate catalyst for our move.

He adopted me the week before Thanksgiving, a few months after the move. By the time the Christmas tree was up, he was raping me. I think the adoption—that validated, legally binding sense of ownership—opened the door in his mind to ownership in another sense: control, possession, free rein.

After experiences like mine—which, of course, I realize are inherently shocking—it seems most people expect dramatic, vivid details: what it felt like, what he said, what I said or did in response. I don't have those details to give. That's not denial or embarrassment talking. If I asked you what you had for breakfast a year ago, you wouldn't remember. This also happened every day, or close to it, so the details are similarly lost. In the case of something this painful, I guess it's a kind of fight-or-flight response. My counselor calls it dissociating—trauma sending the body into protection mode. It has left much of my past as a big, black shadow; I can only see bits and pieces of it.

I can't remember much of anything about the first time he raped me. I'm sure I was hyperaware of every detail at the time, but between the trauma of it and the way it so quickly became the routine, my brain hastily constructed a wall that I can no longer see around. And I don't want to.

I do remember that it didn't hurt after the first couple times, but it certainly wasn't enjoyable. Mostly, I just felt numb. I think I had to be numb. I kind of shut myself down, as if I were in shock—which, I guess, I was. My mind shifted into an odd, detached state to distract my body, or maybe to ignore it entirely.

I remember that while he was raping me, I did a lot of counting. Anything to keep my brain busy. The wooden furniture in their bedroom had patterns of hundreds of tiny holes; they looked like they were made from nails being banged into the wood, but deliberately, delicately so. I became obsessed with them, staring until all the little dots blurred together into one big expanse. I wished it could suck me in, send me tumbling away like Alice down the rabbit hole.

I remember that he used sex as a bargaining tool. If I wanted permission to do something fun with my friends, he'd say, "You have to give me something first." I always knew what that meant. Or if my mom took my cell phone away as punishment for a bad grade, he would offer to get it back for me if I did him some sort of sexual favor first. He did not ask; he told. It all became more and more frequent as I started high school and had more of a social life, and it was always more frequent if I had a boyfriend. Sometimes when I hadn't asked, he would offer afterward to let me hang out with friends, like a reward.

If I said no to his demands, it would be even worse. He would get mad and stop talking to me or make up reasons for me to be grounded. His demeanor toward me would shift so far, so suddenly, that it seemed like everything I did made him angry. I've always been the type of person who can't stand having anyone upset with me. It makes me frantic to make things right. And Mitch's anger toward me had an added consequence: I had become dependent on having him in my corner. So, for him to be the one grounding me or limiting my privileges was disorienting and hurtful. It held a lot of power. Telling him no meant his anger and punishments, yes, but also the larger, dreadful feeling that I would have lost my friend, my dad, and what I perceived as an ally in the battles against my mother.

Their own struggles spilled over into mine. Mom might notice that I had my phone back when I wasn't supposed to. I would tell her that Mitch gave it back to me, and he would say I was lying. These continual head games, layered and clashing with one another, left me feeling paralyzed, powerless, with no sense of what was real.

I remember him telling me he loved me, not like a father would but like a romantic partner would. Despite the control tactics that were an integral part of the abuse, he expressed it as love and affection. And he would try to convince me that I felt the same, saying things like, "You act like I force you to do this. You like it, too!" Clearly, he knew nothing about how I felt, nor did he care. His efforts were blindly persistent, like a hormonal teenage boyfriend trying to get laid.

He was a master of this kind of manipulation, creating his own truth through his words, shaping my perception of the truth. I was a timid kid, trying to understand the workings of the world, and he was the father figure I was supposed to be able to trust to guide me through it all. His words added layers to the confusion already settling in deep from his actions. Did he know better than I did? Did he understand the intricacies of a relationship like ours in ways I couldn't yet? He made it sound like what he was doing to me was fine, perfectly normal, and like I was supposed to be okay with all of it. Like I *was* okay with it. He was telling me not just what to do but what to feel, what to think. My instincts were to fight against all of it, but my confidence in doing so was continually tested, and it exhausted me.

I remember him saying, "Show me your kitty," his weirdly couched term for vagina, as if that took the menace out of it. To this day, that word makes me queasy. Sometimes he would tell me to lift up my shirt. He might touch my breasts, or he might just stare. There didn't have to be physical contact for it to be abuse.

I remember that there was some sort of contact between us nearly every day. Any time we were alone together, it was inevitable. I'm not sure how long any particular incident lasted; I think usually a few minutes. Time is different when you're little. I would be questioned about the timing extensively, years later, in court. As I would tell the attorneys, I wasn't exactly trying to time it out. I was just waiting for it to be over. Whenever it was over, I'd pull up my pants and go back to my bed, or, if he had come into my room, I'd roll over as soon as he'd walked out, keeping my eyes shut tight, and will my mind to find sleep. Once it was over, each time, he was my dad again, and we went on about our normal lives. We went to church and to the movies and to the supermarket as if we were a normal family living a normal life. We didn't speak a word about any of it to anyone.

I remember he would use even a small window of time in the middle of the day, like when Mom would drop me off at home after dance practice and then go back out to pick up Caleb from football. He knew just about how much time he could get away with. He was always on high alert to any sound that might signal her arrival back home, his quick reflexes upon hearing the jingle of keys at the door allowing him to recover and act like nothing had been happening. I would try to avoid him when we were alone, but it would still happen, even if I hadn't asked for any favors, even if I was careful not to make him mad or jealous. It would just happen, for no reason.

It also happened many times when we weren't the only ones home. Sometimes, it even happened in his and my mom's bed while she was sleeping next to us. He would watch her closely for any sign of movement that might mean she was about to wake up. How could she not have known? She must have heard or sensed *something*—if not our movements or his cautious whispers, then the desperate horror radiating from me. But he was very careful, methodical, in his approaches, and she always seemed to be deeply, hopelessly asleep. Maybe she was pretending. I don't know. It was the kind of mattress that, in the commercials, someone can jump on and the wine glass doesn't spill.

I remember always thinking that it would stop soon, that *that* time would be the last time, or that he'd lose interest once I got a little bit older. *Once I turn twelve, it will be over,* I'd think. *Once I turn thirteen.* Then thirteen became fourteen, which became fifteen. And it just kept happening.

I remember that any time I went back to New York to visit Nana and Poppy—an escape I sought out often—intense anxiety would set in a couple days before it was time to go home. I knew what waited for me there, and its contrast with the peace I'd found while away made it even harder to bear. I would cry so hard that it would make me throw up. When Nana would wake me up the morning of Mom's arrival, the tears would start immediately and would continue welling up even as I walked out the door. When any of them asked what was wrong, I couldn't tell them. I feared my tears had revealed too much already, shown too much weakness. I think they thought I just didn't want to leave my grandparents and my hometown, not sure how soon I'd be able to come back, my teenage hormones sending everything into overdrive. No one could have understood the looming dread that only intensified with each mile of road taking me farther from my safety net and closer to the return of the awful daily routine.

Once, I had made myself so sick throughout the entire night before I was supposed to go home that Nana called Mom and said she thought it would be best if I stayed another couple of days, and then she and Poppy would drive me home. She thought it would be unhealthy for me to make such a long car trip in that condition. Mom said she would have to ask Mitch. Nana remembers Mitch saying definitively that I could not stay. Maybe he was getting worried that I was going to tell on him.

Another time, Mitch was going to be picking me up instead of Mom, and I could hardly compose myself. I stowed away in a quiet corner of the kitchen to try to pull myself together, not wanting to let him see me weak and afraid. I wiped at my eyes over and over again, chastising myself, and took several slow, deep breaths, each exhalation coming out in shaky little bursts. I felt like there was no escaping this terrible cycle. I was a prisoner continuing to look for a flaw in the system that could provide my way out, but I was growing more and more frustrated with the search—and with myself— over the years.

I remember that once I started getting my period in middle school, he would rape me anally during that week as a workaround. He had to have known that it was hurting me, because I'd be lying there crying the whole time. He put his hands on my back and told me to hold still, told me it would stop hurting. But it never did. I remember the different texture of that pain, a sharpness that would make it hard to breathe.

I remember that when I had a sore throat, he would tell me that giving him oral sex would make me feel better. The first time he asked me to put it in my mouth, I was so weirded out that I said no, and then I felt such a shameful guilt that I avoided him the rest of the day, worried that I'd only made things worse between us. The things he was asking of me and forcing on me were unspeakable and unforgiveable, and yet, like so many victims, I felt responsible for them.

I was sick so often in those days: severe allergies and congestion, backaches, an irregular heartbeat. My body was expressing the trauma in its own ways, before I could give it a voice. I had an electrocardiogram done, and my mom made me pay for it with the debit card Nana had given me—which was intended to be used for school lunch money—because Mom thought I was faking. She wore her denial like a thick fur coat, wrapping it tight and snuggling into its cozy warmth.

Occasionally, though, the flaws in Mom's elaborate costume would show. She and Mitch would argue late into the night, though I was young enough then that I didn't understand the kind of language they used. I never knew whether one of their fights was something to take seriously or whether it would blow over by morning. One argument started after one of the many times she seemed to have found us out; I was getting dressed in their bedroom while Mitch was in the adjoining master bathroom, and Mom pounded on the door as she shouted questions about what he was doing in there. She *must* have known. Sometimes their fights got physical. Once, Mom had left a deep scratch on Mitch's neck, and he threatened to press charges. But that was nothing compared to the time I saw him drag her down the hallway by her hair.

She had packed her bags to leave him several times. She threatened to move back to New York with Caleb and me, sending Mitch into a panic. They came tantalizingly close to a legal separation. She asked me how I would feel if the two of them lived in separate places. I remember such a jarring discord of emotions: I was sad about the idea of my family being split up, but in the same instant there was a rush of relief, imagining being free from Mitch and his gruff hands and his burnt-plastic stench. The mere thought of no longer living with him made the tightness in my chest disintegrate, just for a moment, and scatter away like marbles.

But she would always change her mind and stay.

Even if somehow my mom had been oblivious to what Mitch was doing to me, if somehow she had remained in denial as the trial began, if she didn't *want* to believe it, it should have been impossible to ignore or forgive how awkwardly Mitch danced around denying the allegations. If you were accused of despicable crimes you did not commit, in a trial tearing apart your family, with the tension permeating every room you entered, every ounce of air you struggled to breathe, wouldn't you be absolutely, adamantly sure to emphasize that you were innocent? That there was no way you could even fathom the allegations? You probably would be horrified and ask a lot of confused questions when the detectives came knocking at your door. You probably would feel devastated, a mixture of speechless, pleading, and determinedly convincing. You probably would offer up something more than, "I don't know what to say."

And yet my mother continued—still continues—to insist that Mitch was innocent. I have spent so many years wondering how anyone could be so persistently blind to the truth—whether she truly didn't see it or had deliberately put up blinders so she didn't have to face it. So she could ignore it. Sometimes I do think she was just afraid of the truth, or she had waited too long to question him and then was in too deep to change course. But part of me still wonders if she did truly come to believe him. Maybe she was brainwashed, taken in under his spell, rather than making an intentional choice against me. Otherwise, I don't know how she could tell lie after damaging lie, at least if she has any kind of conscience. But I'm never quite sure.

Either way, I think Mom loved Mitch so much that she wasn't willing to turn against him.

I wanted her to love *me* that much.

Even after a jury convicted Mitch on thirteen counts, even after he has now spent nearly eight years in prison and is registered as a violent sex offender, Mom continues to wait for reality to match her way of thinking, rather than catching up the other way around. She keeps waiting for him, and she keeps me closed off. She's constructed a door between us that has remained closed, locked, and bulletproof. I spent years fighting against it with my full weight, calling to her until my voice wore out. But she refused to listen.

Ghost Stories

When I was little and would get scared at night, my mom would let me come to bed with her and Mitch. As I got older and that need faded, Mitch created the fear, to try to recreate that need. Early on, I had turned to him because I was seeking comfort from the anxieties that plagued me in the still darkness of night—not knowing he had created the entire situation as the perfect opportunity to abuse me. The physical assaults and the mind games went hand in hand. He tried to convince me that there was a ghost in our apartment. At night, I would be startled awake by something running through the room or a pillow being thrown at me. He would creep in and turn on my TV in the middle of the night, filling my bedroom with a burst of light and sound. I wouldn't say it was fear that he created at first, but confusion, disorientation. And he played on that.

Caleb and I would often sleep on the floor in each other's rooms. My bed had a trundle bed that tucked away underneath when not in use but was frequently pulled out to the middle of the floor, with Caleb and his Tennessee Titans blankets taking up residence. The two of us had shared a bedroom while living in New York, so it was our routine, our comfort zone, and I didn't like being alone—which, of course, only got worse as Mitch began his patterns of abuse, leaving me rattled. Any time I was alone at night, I was hyperaware of every noise, every shadow, and fought to keep my eyes open, knowing how often falling asleep meant falling deep into a fitful nightmare. But Caleb's camping out in my room was an obstacle for Mitch's plans. Eventually, he told me to let my brother sleep on his own because I was annoying him, though I hadn't heard any complaints from Caleb.

So I started going back into my parents' bedroom instead, sleeping on a quilt on the floor. Their room seemed like the safer place to go, despite the fact that Mitch's presence brought its own threats. Being afraid for a few minutes is a lot better than being afraid all night by yourself.

There wasn't enough space on Mom's side of the room, so I was always on the side next to Mitch. He would hang his arm down off the side of the bed and grope at me. I would pretend I was still asleep, thinking maybe that would make him stop. I would cough, or roll over and kick a leg out so that it hit the dresser—trying to make a noise loud enough to wake my mother but natural enough not to raise Mitch's suspicions. He would often invite me up into the bed to sleep right next to him. He would hold me and caress me, getting bolder as time went on, testing the waters to see how much he could get away with without Mom noticing. It turned out the answer was a lot.

Before too long, I had figured out that the "ghost" was a man-made façade, because if I didn't respond the way Mitch wanted, the alleged hauntings would escalate. If a thrown pillow didn't send me running to him for comfort, next there would be tapping on the wall. This specter was quite persistent in wanting me afraid. But even once I knew it was all a matter of Mitch's manipulation, I felt powerless to stop it. It was like I was in a trance, and *knew* I was, but wasn't able to snap out of it. Like a dream you can't make yourself wake up from. I felt numb and weakened and hopeless.

There's a scene in the Netflix series *13 Reasons Why* that is seared into my memory for its heart-stopping accuracy. We viewers learn through flashbacks what led up to protagonist Hannah's suicide; the family and friends mourning her death can't fathom what led her to that drastic decision, and we put the puzzle pieces together as they do. By the time she finds herself in the hot tub with Bryce, she's suffered a number of betrayals from people she thought she could trust and has had her self-confidence shaken to the point that it's irreparably broken. She is a shell of a girl, barely keeping it together. When Bryce first starts kissing her and touching her in this pivotal scene, she tries to stop him. She tells him no. She makes it clear with her voice and her body that she isn't interested. But it doesn't even faze him.

We see her experience irritation, frustration, panic, and eventually that same hopelessness and numbness I felt so many times myself. When he turns her around and rapes her, her chest and arms laid over the edge of the hot tub just as mine were on the bed, we can see in her face that she has no fight left. Her face seems expressionless, but those vacant eyes scream a level of hurt that cannot otherwise be expressed. Those eyes haunt me. I knew them as my own from the moment I first saw the episode and felt my entire body turn to ice. The showrunners and actress got it exactly right: those are the eyes of someone who has given up, who wants desperately to be anywhere other than where she is in that endless moment but knows the only way to get there is to let her mind leave her body, to lessen the trauma in any increment possible.

I remember Mom yelling at Mitch a few times about having me sleep in their bed, saying I was too old to do so. It sounded more like annoyance than concern. She didn't seem to like my being there, but she didn't press and ask the bigger questions: why he wanted me there, why he encouraged it, why I was always lying so close to him. She must have had suspicions, but she stopped asking after those early-on questions about inappropriate touching, questions I hadn't known how to answer. It was like we were never ready to open that door at the same time, and after those early, halfhearted attempts, she insisted on keeping that door shut and locked. She didn't want to know. She would pretend there was nothing hiding behind it.

I knew from a young age—stretching back to when we were still living in New York—that there was some tension between Mom and Mitch about sex. Mom often seemed like she didn't trust him and was looking to catch him about something. She asked me to help her find out what he had been looking at online. I didn't know what sorts of things she was looking for, but when I found the search history option, a lot of nasty things showed up. I often saw him looking at those kinds of websites over the years, including long after we'd moved to Tennessee and I'd become far too familiar with his sexual preferences. I never said anything about it, to him or to my mom, because somehow it always felt like I would be the one to get in trouble.

So there had long been an unsettling air around the entire topic of sex in relation to Mitch and my mom. Only long after the fact did I come to realize how inappropriate it was for Mom to involve me in that. At the time, I just knew that I didn't really understand it and that it made me feel weird—which then extended into Mitch's sexual actions toward me. It was all so taboo and confusing and embarrassing. I never knew how to verbalize the questions I had and ultimately felt like I shouldn't.

Once, while Caleb was still camped out on my bedroom floor, Mitch threw a shoe toward my bed in the middle of the night and missed his target, hitting Caleb instead. Freaked out by it, Caleb said something about it to Mom the next day, and she just dismissed it. I told him, "Don't worry; it's just Dad."

Mom seemed to think (or at least acted like) that was a strange conclusion for me to have arrived at. "Why would you say something like that?" she asked, accusatorily, condescendingly.

I backed off and told her I had only said it to make Caleb feel better.

Again and again, I still find myself wondering: why would she not be surprised or concerned by any of that? Why would she not investigate? The only answer I can think of is that there's no need to investigate when you already know the answer.

Eventually, Mom moved me to a different bedroom, farther away from theirs.

And when I stopped going into my parents' room for comfort, Mitch would come to mine.

In many ways, Mitch did succeed in creating ghosts that haunted me, ones I still can't quite dismiss. I'm twenty-four, and I live with my grandparents. I sleep with a light on, sharing my bed with a worn-out Bible, a stuffed cat, and my coonhound mix, Bella. I have Christmas lights strung up around my window that I keep plugged in year-round. I often leave the TV on at night as well, so I don't have to wonder if it will turn on by itself. If it's not on, it's unplugged. The sound of a creaking floorboard can send me into night terrors. I have double locks on my bedroom door, and Nana and Poppy had a security alarm system installed in the house. Sometime after the trial ended, I was finally able to talk myself into leaving my bedroom to shower regularly or even to use the toilet—I had started peeing in my pants in sixth grade, shortly after the abuse started, and found it a horrifyingly hard habit to break, well into young adulthood. I couldn't quiet the fear that someone was going to come after me. That lurking feeling, a tickle up my spine, followed me everywhere. Even with Mitch in prison. Maybe he would send someone else to track me down.

Still today, I rarely use the back door of the house, especially after dark, because I can too easily imagine Mitch coming up behind me. I hear his voice questioning and coercing over the tiniest things. In the summer, my friends wear low-rise shorts that show a little midriff, but I censor myself, afraid of what Mitch would say, or do, if he saw me wearing them: he'd forbid me to leave the house like that, all the while drinking the sight in for himself. My rational mind knows he's not around, but it still feels like he's looking.

Of all the many demons the abuse created, the most persistent is the one that torments my romantic relationships. I dated a few guys in high school, most of them casual, one that would prove crucial in my fight against Mitch, and one that lasted a bit longer, continuing after we'd graduated. All of those relationships were part of my life during some combination of the investigation, trial, and ongoing aftermath. It was hard, or maybe impossible, to expect those guys—those *boys*, really—to catch up to the seriousness of it all, the weight of it. We were so young.

The abuse had been a part of my life for so long, almost as far back as I could remember. I'd had time to at least start processing what had happened, to grapple with the terribleness of it, including the fact that I had no idea how long the terribleness would last or what new levels of it might be coming. These boys who came into my life were not prepared to take all of that on, and I can't blame them. They tried. The infinite questions, awkwardness, and anger that an abusive past inevitably stirs up are daunting for any one person to manage. To co-manage them alongside someone else's processing can feel insurmountable. I know this has been true for me and am sure it must have been true for them.

Of course, it was often helpful to have a boyfriend to talk to as I worked to sort through all of it. They were among the very few people I felt I *could* talk to about it. Some learned more than others; some just surface level and some maybe much deeper and rawer than they were ready to go. At times I didn't know how honest *I* was ready to be until the words started pouring out of me like bathwater spilling over the edge of the tub. This all has continued through my dating life in my twenties. My teenage baggage is much harder to outgrow than the typical anguish of puberty.

No matter what level I've been able to attain with any guy emotionally, attempting to be close with someone physically has felt nearly impossible. To be intimate and affectionate and trusting is difficult when the entire idea of physical intimacy was introduced to me by someone who had no right to it, leaving anything related to the topic tainted. Sex in general feels dirty and wrong, and I have blocks built in that I can't quiet. There are moments when I'll have to stop the momentum and blurt out, "Don't do that." Most of the time, I think I wouldn't care if I never had sex again in my life. I'm sick of the whole idea.

The effects trickle down to tiny details, too: something a guy says that reminds me of something Mitch said, or even the simple fact that Mitch and a guy I dated both liked barbecue chicken. (The smell of barbecue sauce is an immediate, instinctive trigger for me. I can't stomach it.) It's like I hold grudges against guys for things they never did, never would do. Once, a guy I was seeing innocently ran through the room in the dark, and I flashed back to Mitch's scare tactics and started hitting him. I hate when anybody whispers in my ear. My body instinctively associates it with hushed encounters with Mitch in the dark. It doesn't matter that my brain knows it's not Mitch lying next to me, that it's someone I do want affection from; it still makes me shudder. It causes an immediate, all-encompassing sense of something like panic, where a shiver will course through my whole body like I'm suddenly freezing. I have to work consciously to distract myself and reroute my thoughts—all while trying not to kill the mood, which is no small task. So many mental tricks, just like the old days. I fear no partner will ever fully understand the countless triggers, no matter how much I try to explain them. Sometimes I'm not up for trying.

The dirtiness I feel leaves me self-conscious, like the abuse stained me. My brain tries to compensate for that with a sometimes overwhelming need to be perfect. It's a compulsion. My clothes, my hair, my makeup, my nails, my body, everything—it's a way to keep control over *something*. But I can scrub my skin for hours and never feel clean. I sculpt my face with careful contours and bright lipstick, all with studied precision, but I see only what I'm covering up.

Trust is a huge issue for me in all relationships, whether romantic or with friends. Tell me the sky is blue, and I'll still go outside and check. After so many years of not feeling safe in my own home, I can't help but always be alert and guarded. It's not something I actively think about; it's not like I think *I'd better be careful* or ask myself *Can I trust this person?* It's just instinctive, robotic. It leaves me feeling lonely even when I'm with other people. It's like I'm living in a world that runs parallel to the one everyone else lives in; I can see that other track but can't quite get onto it.

I love going running, but I can't bring myself to run past the cemetery in town. I don't want to go near a place so heavy with loss and eeriness; I feel haunted as it is, everywhere I go. Instead, I make up awkward routes to avoid it. If I even get close to it, my body tenses up in impending panic. It's hard to go out at all, especially in our small town, with all the places I try to avoid. My grandparents' house is right around the corner from where my family and I lived when I was a kid. So many of my mom's and Mitch's friends live nearby, and for a while some of them even worked at the same company I did. I often feel like I'm being watched. Even family friends I grew up with feel like enemies now or, perhaps worse, strangers—people I don't really know anymore and wouldn't feel comfortable trying to get reacquainted with. It's clear they see me differently because of what was done to me, and the thought of trying to change that perspective, or that it should even be my responsibility to do so, is exhausting.

While it can be tempting to stay shut in, I don't like being home alone, either. When I am, I don't leave my bedroom. I can't handle all the empty space around me. This is especially hard for friends my age to grasp, since most early-twentysomethings relish their independence. My fears are as nonsensical to them as a fear of heights is to a rollercoaster junkie like me. There's no way to make them understand how deep the roots of that fear reach. Its vines course through my veins like an infection, unstoppable and stubborn.

Once, I went to a bonfire in a friend's backyard. A few people in the group were telling ghost stories, and I started to feel panicked. Even though I knew they were only stories and that my clammy, chest-tightening reaction was trauma based, I still couldn't shut it off. I thought maybe if I just played around on my phone for a while, I could tune them out. But my mind was right back in my childhood bedroom, tensing up from neck to knees in anticipation of the TV blaring on or a pillow being thrown or those stomach-churning whispers and invasive hands. I shot up, interrupting one of them mid-sentence by saying, "I think it's time to go." My seemingly sudden change of heart as my anxiety boiled over made the group think I was mad at them. Several of them called after me as I retreated out front to my car.

A friend who knew about my past told me later that he'd tried to make light of it after I'd left, telling the others that I got freaked out easily by stories like that—but now that's made it a joke among them, one they think I can laugh along with, not knowing how it makes my stomach ache. "Careful, Jessica, the ghost will get you!"

I can never make them understand the ghosts that do haunt me.

I often don't want to try. I generally don't like to tell people too much about my past. That's hard when your story is a mere Google search away. It was especially hard at fifteen years old, when the news first broke and I felt like I was walking around with headlines plastered all over my body. The pitying looks don't get any easier to handle over time. And with my friends in particular, I don't want it to be a defining factor of our relationships.

On the other hand, sometimes it's even harder when someone *doesn't* know my story. A woman at work stopped me one day and told me she was my aunt. I had seen her at work every day for months, not knowing of any connection. It was such a bizarre feeling—detached and floating away, like I was watching it happen to someone else.

"Do you remember me?" she asked. Then, after an awkward pause that felt like it loitered for minutes: "You really don't?"

She seemed hurt, or at least greatly confused. I felt guilty and yet knew the fault wasn't mine, which was a disorienting mix. I knew my mom must not have told this woman any piece of the story, not given her any explanation for our disappearance from her life. She must have distanced herself from this sister when the investigation first started, just as she had from so many other people who had cared about her. About me.

Because of that, so many pieces of my life are missing. My mother holds them hostage and left me not even knowing what had been taken. She left me to find out for myself, in waves.

Perhaps the worst part about that achingly awkward conversation with my newly discovered aunt was that, when I got home that night, I wished I could pick up the phone and call my mom about it. It's moments like that, when conversation seems necessary and yet isn't an option, that I feel my mom's absence most palpably. It's like the echo of a voice that was just speaking a moment ago, or a presence that I turned toward as it left the room, just a second too late. More apparitions. More ghosts.

I did try to contact my mother once. I texted her to say I missed her and Caleb. I was aware of my fingers quivering as I typed the message. It was like I was reaching out to a stranger.

Mom's reply said not to contact her unless I'm ready to come out with the truth.

People often ask me what I'll do if my mom reaches out to me someday. I'm never sure how to answer that, because my instinctive, childlike reaction of wanting my mother doesn't make sense if I pause long enough to look at reality. I would certainly be timid at first, and suspicious. My mom has always been highly manipulative (she and Mitch are astonishingly matched in that sense), and I found it hard to determine her intentions most of the time. If I was immersed in a book, she would read the last few chapters and tell me how it ended. She did this with the last book in the Harry Potter series, disintegrating the realm of wizardry and mystery I'd escaped to and dragging me back to the harsh reality from which no fantasy could release me. Once, when I had just gotten a new purse from Nana, Mom dumped everything out of it when I left the room. Sometimes, she would take money out of my purse when I wasn't around and then claim that I must have spent it, when I knew I hadn't. She liked to play head games. She would call me to say she'd be home in twenty minutes, and then she'd walk through the door right afterward, looking to catch me covering up something. There was nothing for her to uncover, until, of course, the later years, when I wished she *would* have walked in sooner.

My mother had a long history of unhealthy relationships, the pregnancy and subsequent breakup with my father being far from the first example. Poppy says Mom has always seen herself as number one and everyone else as a distant second. While she was pregnant with me, she was only seventeen and not well suited for motherhood. Nana and Poppy had offered to adopt me. They were ready to sign the papers, and then Mom changed her mind. How different my life could have been!

Despite that change of plans, Nana and Poppy did help my mom out a lot in raising me, and Nana in particular grew very attached to me from the beginning. I'm aware of many references by my mother to me being "the favorite"—a term that always had a bit of an edge to it. Though I never quite understood the tension surrounding it, at least not as a kid, my closeness with Nana seemed to be a further catalyst for conflict. Mom thought Nana was controlling in terms of how I was raised. Once Caleb came along, two and a half years later, there was an added layer of tension. The close bond Nana had fostered with me set a high bar, so Mom often complained that things weren't fair to Caleb, and she'd use that as an excuse to keep Nana and Poppy away.

Mom *always* seemed to be entrenched in some form of turmoil with Nana, whether about Caleb and me or any number of other things. When I think back to my childhood, it was more common for them not to be talking. They had silences between them that lasted years. While many of my friends talked of family visits to their grandparents' houses, especially at the holidays, that just wasn't a part of my world. The weird thing is my mom had always said she and I would break the curse of mothers and daughters not getting along, which she had seen in earlier generations as well as among her friends and their mothers. It seemed to be a sort of epidemic, and she wanted to find the cure. Or at least she said she did.

I don't expect to hear from my mom anytime soon. For a while, during the trial and even afterward, I did catch myself hoping she would show up at our door. Sometimes I'd picture her apologizing, having had some sort of awakening and real-izing that Mitch was the one she should have cast out. Other times I'd picture her still closed off or unsure, but even in those fantasies I was relieved to see her and eager to let her in. I would have taken any contact, any chance. Maybe I still would. Maybe that's why I use the same Tide laundry deter-gent she did, still linger in the cleaning-products aisle, breathing in the fabric softeners, slowly, eyes closed, trying to pinpoint the exact scent that conjures her and home and comfort, that mends the tie there used to be between *home* and *comfort*. Those visions of opening the door to see her standing on the porch started fading a long time ago, but I can't seem to let go of them completely.

I *do* still anticipate Mitch coming to the door. He only has two years left of his sentence, at most. He's appealed a few times, and each time I feel like I'm closed in a small box with no air, until the denial verdict comes through and I can move and breathe normally again. What will happen when he's released? Will he come looking for me? Try to talk to me? Try to make a fresh start—or to start the cycle all over again?

I'm always a little on edge, expecting the ghost to come knocking.

Caught in the Act

I WASN'T THE ONE WHO TOLD. NOT DIRECTLY, ANYWAY. I have to wonder how much longer the abuse would have gone on if Aaron, my tenth-grade boyfriend, hadn't spoken up when he did. If any link in the chain of communication—me to Aaron to his mom to our pastor to the police—had faltered, how much more time would have passed? How much more damage done?

Though there were plenty of times I'd wished I could scream the truth in my mother's face, or pull aside a friend or a teacher or *anyone* and beg them to hear me, I was too afraid to actually take that step, to make the cataclysmic shift from thought to action, because I knew my family would be shaken forever if I did. Maybe this secret was mine to carry, in order to protect my mom and brother. It was such a nauseating paradox: I couldn't stomach the thought of remaining in the status quo, always knowing that Mitch's touch and breath and panting thrusts were lurking, yet the alternate path didn't seem like a lesser evil. I didn't feel that the crushing weight of this burden would get any lighter by sharing it.

Yet it *was* suffocating to carry it alone. Sometimes I was surprised people couldn't sense it on me somehow: see a quiet chaos in my eyes or a tension in the way I walked. Sometimes I felt so scarred and dirty that it seemed people must be able to see it, smell it, hear it screaming from my bones. Yes, I was afraid to break up my family, to speak aloud the things that had happened in quiet, darkened rooms. But I was afraid every day already—afraid I would say the wrong thing, ask the wrong way, wear the wrong clothes. Afraid he would want more. Afraid the sickening carousel was never going to stop. Maybe I was ready for a different kind of fear.

I guess I found a compromise in telling Aaron enough that he drew the right conclusions; I told him without having to say the words directly. The night that became such a pivotal moment in all our lives, the point of no return, started out simple and unassuming. I certainly had no idea at the time that we all, along with detectives and attorneys and other people I had yet to meet, would be dissecting the details of that night for years to come.

I invited Aaron over to watch a movie on a Friday night. We were a couple of fifteen-year-old kids, excited just to be hanging out on our own in the living room, cuddling on the couch, eating popcorn, making out. We went to different schools but the same church and youth group, and we'd been boyfriend and girlfriend for about four months at that time. It was the first time I'd had a boy come over. My mom was in Africa on a mission trip and wouldn't be back for a few more days. Aaron's visit never would have happened with her home. It was fall break from school, so Caleb and I had been home all week, although he stayed with Mitch's parents, Grandpa John and Grandma Sally, for much of that time. Mitch was off of work. He told Mom he'd decided to take the time off to make sure I wouldn't have Aaron over during the day, unsupervised. Really, that meant Mitch and I had had a lot of time alone together, which of course he utilized thoroughly. I had grown increasingly tense and tired throughout the week; the numbness I was typically able to rely on was wearing away from the heightened frequency of it all.

Mitch watched a movie in his bedroom with Caleb that night but made his presence known, leaving his door open and sending Caleb out every twenty minutes or so, under the guise of getting them more drinks or snacks. Mitch's watchfulness felt less like a protective parent and more like a predator stalking its prey.

When I went to refill our sodas in the kitchen, separated from the living room by a breakfast bar, Mitch was waiting there by the fridge, like a parent might who's ready to give their kid a talking-to. But I knew there would be no words.

He came up behind me, his body pressed against mine, uncomfortably warm; the room felt smaller, closing in. With his arms like vises at my sides, he slid his hands up over my shirt—which suddenly felt uselessly thin—and cupped my breasts. I could hear my heartbeat in my ears and feel it in an unyielding lump in my throat when I tried to usher in more air. Had we burned the popcorn? Something was burning, smoky, stale, toxic. I wanted to cough but was afraid to make a sound. I wanted to throw up. To cry. To yell to Aaron. Instead, I stared across the room at the back of his head and silently urged him to turn around and see.

And he did.

When I first saw Aaron sit up straighter on the couch to peer over from across the room, I was startled; had I actually said his name out loud? I felt a twinge of dread in anticipating how Mitch would react. But no, I hadn't made a sound; I was well accustomed to keeping my protests silent, dissociating, studying the ceiling tiles. As Aaron told me later, he had simply been wondering if I was making my way back yet and was startled himself to see something that he couldn't quite identify but knew instinctively wasn't right. He would later tell detectives that he was thinking, "There's no way that I just saw that," his brain scrambling to come up with other explanations for what could have been happening.

Mitch saw Aaron see us and pulled away. There is no natural way to behave after something like that, though—whether you pretend you were doing something else or pretend nothing happened, it's clearly an act. This was new territory; no one had seen before. Before, he would simply walk away and I would adjust my clothes and we'd go about our day as if everything were normal. Before, I could try to suppress it like a bad dream or a hallucination. Now, it was real. It was known.

I attempted the nonchalant charade for the rest of the movie, avoiding Aaron's probing looks and his carefully whispered "Everything okay?" The movie ended shortly afterward, and he tried calling his friend for a ride home but wasn't able to reach him. He asked me if Mitch could drive him instead. He couldn't have known, of course, just what he was asking of me. Favors always came at a cost.

The incident in the kitchen had rattled me, these two worlds intersecting. I felt nervous in a more palpable way than I usually did; it bubbled closer to the surface. Maybe that's what finally allowed me to say as much as I did.

Aaron asked me if Mitch would be mad about having to drive him home.

"If he's mad," I answered, "he won't be mad for long. He'll make me make him happy."

We just sat there for a minute, the silence swelling between us. Aaron's stare revealed how hard his mind was trying to make sense of all of this and to deny the conclusions he was arriving at. He asked me what I meant.

"What do you think it means?" I said, again telling without telling.

I later found out that Aaron was suspicious of Mitch before I said anything. He said he'd noticed that the way Mitch would look at me wasn't the way a father looks at a daughter. But I didn't know that in that moment, of course, and it felt like an accident that I was saying anything at all, like my brain couldn't catch up to my mouth and shut it up.

I hoped I was saying enough that Aaron would tell someone else, someone who could help. I trusted him in a way I'd never trusted anyone. I felt he could be my anchor. At the same time, I was afraid about how much I was saying, even in those cryptic snippets. Maybe it *was* enough, which was more than I'd ever said about it to anyone. Maybe it was too much.

I wanted him to tell. I was terrified that he would tell.

Mitch did give Aaron a ride home that night. Caleb and I rode along with them. No one said a word the entire drive. The awkwardness couldn't be ignored; the silence announced it persistently. The tension was like humidity.

As we left Aaron's house, Mitch grabbed my cell phone from me and tossed it up on the dashboard of the truck, where it slid around as he made each turn, sharply, pointedly. Mitch's eyes tracing its movements were like eyes on me, burning, accusing.

We dropped Caleb off at Grandpa John and Grandma Sally's apartment for the night. When we got home, I sat on the couch, quiet and still, like a stunned animal. My brain hadn't caught up to processing all that had just unfolded, and I couldn't quite make sense of the strange cocktail of emotions churning through me. There was some level of relief from having finally told someone, but it was mixed with shock and fear and denial. (Had it even really happened? What had I said, exactly? Did Aaron understand?) There was also a bit of hope. And exhaustion. And sadness.

Mitch came in, turned on the TV, and sat at the other end of the couch. We didn't look at each other or speak. I could feel my heartbeat in the sides of my throat and had to concentrate to swallow; my pulse was a wiggling lump, getting in the way.

I was afraid to ask for my phone back, or to try to apologize about Aaron needing a ride unexpectedly, or to say or do anything.

Eventually, so tired I could hardly keep my eyes open, I forced myself to stand up and head to bed. Mitch cleared his throat loudly, freezing me in place as if he'd flipped a control switch.

"Why don't you sleep next to me tonight," he said. It was not a question.

All I wanted was some space, a chance to finally fall into the type of deep sleep I'd gone months—or maybe years—without. I needed a break from the commotion in my head and the jittery buzzing of my nerves.

But I knew there was no choice, and that resisting or arguing would only make things worse.

Looking back on it, I realize that, to other people, it might seem illogical that Mitch told me to sleep with him that night —he was angry with me, and we had barely spoken since leaving to take Aaron home. But his anger was an integral part of his control. They were intertwined so tightly that I often couldn't tell them apart.

38

I can't remember if he abused me that night. Certainly, the threat of it would have been there constantly, as it always was. He had made me sleep in his bed every night while Mom had been away. He was still expecting that of me.

He kept my phone away from me until the next day, I guess assuming that the pressing need for conversation would have faded by then. Taking the phone away was a control tactic—and giving it back felt like a dare.

It was a risk I was willing to take. In Aaron, I finally had someone I could confide in about these things that had remained unspoken for years too long. He hadn't judged me or dismissed what I was saying as impossible. He believed me. He wanted to help me. He was angry at Mitch, not at me. I had been so afraid of speaking up that this outcome was genuinely a surprise; as much as I liked and trusted Aaron, I had lost trust in the world around me to the point that I thought I would always be in this fight alone. The ability to ease even a tiny bit of this burden with the press of a few buttons was intoxicatingly soothing. I grabbed on to that life-line with desperate hope.

Aaron and I talked more that weekend, whenever we could get away with it in privacy, and with each conversation I found myself opening up a bit more, loosening the choke-hold and allowing myself to share some of those terrible truths.

We talked about telling my mom, but I confessed my fear to him about tearing apart my family. How could I willingly make that choice? The current suffering was a known enemy. I didn't want it to continue tormenting me, but the alternative seemed even more sinister somehow.

I asked him not to tell anyone, which I realize now was a hell of a request. But it was so new and disorienting to have even one person know, and I was afraid of letting this thing snowball and roll away from me before I was ready. Would I ever be ready, though? Eventually, maybe just to quiet his anxiety for the short term, I told Aaron that I would tell my mom about it when she got home from Africa in a few days. I guess I wanted to hold onto some semblance of control.

Then, the Monday after "movie night" (as it would soon come to be known throughout months of analysis and debate), Mitch raped me for the last time. In that moment, of course, I couldn't have imagined it would be the last; I felt as numb as I always did, powerless and destined to repeat this cycle. I wanted to hang out with Aaron that night, and in order to do so, there was a toll to pay. It had all become practically automatic. Mitch had told me to go in his room and wait for him, more of a direction than a coaxing or a threat. It was all so routine, so matter of fact. He came in and bent me over the bed. My feet could hardly touch the floor. I stared at the mirror on the bedroom wall and counted the swirls carved into its wooden frame until Mitch was through and had retreated into the bathroom. I pulled my pants up, went to my own room and got my phone, and texted Aaron: "It happened again."

I don't know if I honestly thought things could continue as they were, or if I believed they would stop on their own, or if I just needed not to be the one to pull the alarm. Regardless, in hindsight, I think I'm glad Aaron felt he had to speak up, and that he was willing to be that voice for me when I couldn't quite summon my own.

I still have to say I *think* I'm glad he told, because I quickly learned how right I was about the enemy lurking around that next corner. The hell I was about to face gave the hell I'd been through a run for its money.

Aaron told his mother what he knew. They debated

waiting to tell anyone else until my mom got back from her trip, but Aaron was too distraught, and they realized that any night they waited could be another night it happened. His mom talked to her sister for advice. Together, they called our pastor. He called the police.

I picture this chain of conversation like a forest fire: beginning with one small spark that succumbs to the heat, soon engulfing everything in its path.

As scary as that ripple effect was—like a tear in a seam that you can't stop from unraveling—I knew on some level even then that the truth did need to come out, not only to stop this awful cycle in my own life but also for some greater good. At that time, it was just a vague awareness, somewhere out on the periphery, a call I couldn't yet fully hear. But there were little snippets of a bigger picture forming. For instance, I'd started to worry what would happen if I had kids someday and they went to Mitch's house. That made my stomach drop to an even greater depth than it did from all that I had already endured personally. I knew it had to stop. It would stop now. It would stop with me.

Later, in court, Mitch's lawyer would try to argue that I had invented my entire line of accusations because Aaron and I got caught fooling around on the couch that night and I was afraid of getting in trouble. They portrayed me as promiscuous, looking to get some action but afraid to own up to it. In reality, all I knew of sex was what Mitch had taught me through experiences I had no desire to repeat, not with him or Aaron or anyone else. Any curiosity that may swell up in the average hormonal teenager had been stripped away for me; the mystery and allure of sex were gone. I knew sex only as a chore, a consequence.

There was a horrible irony to the defense's argument that

Mitch was on trial simply because I was embarrassed for having gotten frisky with my boyfriend and gotten caught. I wish I'd had the opportunity to make impulsive decisions like that, to choose whether or not I was ready for sex. I wish I only had to dread the *usual* sex talks between teenagers and their parents, arguing that I was ready and wanted to get condoms or the pill, insisting that my boyfriend was *the one*. Or that I could have decided I wasn't ready and maybe struggled through temptations in order to hold myself to it. To choose to be a virgin for my husband.

When I was around thirteen or fourteen years old, a series of guest speakers had visited youth group to talk to the girls about the importance of waiting until marriage to have sex. I don't know if the boys were also preached to about sex, but I know they went outside to play games while we had our classes and prepared for an abstinence ceremony. We all bought white dresses and special rings. My ring was from JCPenney, a silver band engraved with the words *purity* and *love*, fancy enough to be purchased from the jewelry counter with all the locked cases on it. And then we sat with our families in a big room set up with tables all around it, like at a wedding reception, and each girl stood up, turned to face her father, and pledged that she would remain abstinent until she was married. We were each given a little card to sign with the pledge printed on it. As I recited the words, I remember thinking, *How can I promise this? I'm pledging to be abstinent—except for with my dad, apparently?* I was being taught that sex was something I wasn't supposed to do, but it had been being done to me for years. I wanted the words to be true, wanted to be able to make that vow and be a part of that special moment we'd all been working toward. But I was trying to promise something that Mitch had already taken away from me. And he sat there watching me, letting me speak those words to him in front of everyone, knowing that he had forced me into that lie.

Because of him, I didn't have the freedom to be abstinent, nor to have frisky dates and rushes of hormones and birds-and-bees talks. I didn't have a choice.

Speaking My Truth

I.

Four days after I had first told Aaron about the abuse, the day after that final incident, Detectives Tommy Roberts and Wayne Lawson knocked on our front door. Wayne knew Mitch from having coached a couple years of Little League football together, and he had met me before, briefly. His ex-wife was a good friend of Mom's. I think those connections were why Tommy was also involved and would ultimately be the lead detective on the case. When Tommy first walked into my room to talk with me that night, I had no idea I was gaining a much-needed protector. He would be by my side throughout the new ordeal that was about to begin.

It was—or, rather, it had been—mostly a typical Tuesday. I had gone to school but had come home early, feeling sick to my stomach. I'd taken a nap and woke up feeling better. I had largely avoided Mitch, so there hadn't been an opportunity for him to abuse me. It helped that I hadn't asked permission to do anything with my friends. But he had raped me the night before, which is what I had texted Aaron about.

I was doing homework on my bed and talking to Aaron on the phone when there was a knock on my bedroom door. Tommy introduced himself as a detective with the local police department. Other than the badge hanging from a cord around his neck, I wouldn't have known he was a police officer; he was wearing a T-shirt, cargo shorts, and a baseball cap. He looked like a dad who'd just come in from playing a game of catch. His entire demeanor gave off a trustworthy vibe, although my instinct was to question that. When he asked if I knew why he was there, I could feel how wide my eyes were, unblinking, and couldn't seem to find my voice. I just nodded yes. He asked if there was any truth to it, and I nodded again. He decided we should talk further at the police station—he later told me he wanted to get me away from the scene of the abuse as quickly as possible—and arranged to have a female officer come pick me up.

I found myself in a cop car for the first (and only) time in my life. The glimmer of protection I felt upon getting in was overshadowed by an uneasiness, which had started with the sight of the cars in our driveway and Tommy at my door. This was real. People were talking about it; I was talking about it. Consequences were being set into motion, and there could be no turning back now.

Tommy reassured me from the beginning, and continually throughout our many months of conversations, that I hadn't done anything wrong and that the most important thing to him was that I tell the truth. He said nothing I would tell him would shock him; he'd been in this line of work a long time and had to have many conversations like this. I took that as his way of trying to make me feel more at ease. Still, telling him—a man I had just met, who was as old as or older than my father, with children of his own—about the things that had been done to me was so uncomfortable. I was fifteen years old. I blushed using the words "penis" and "vagina." I tried to be vague at first, using words like "it" and "there," but Tommy needed to know specifics: what Mitch touched or inserted and where; what I defined as "sex." I was so young and timid that when he asked me if there had been anal intercourse, I had to ask what that was. I had experienced it but didn't have a name for it. But yes, I told him with wide eyes, it hurt. I didn't know the word "erection," either. I had just called it "hard." Tommy helped me to understand how important it was for him to know the details and that Mitch's defense team would ask me about these same things in less delicate ways when the case proceeded to court. In addition to completing his own procedural duties, he was preparing me.

I told him, slowly, in response to each probing question, that Mitch would kiss me, not just on the mouth but on my neck and my breasts and inside my legs. I told him that Mitch would touch my vagina but not insert his fingers. That he first put his penis in my vagina in sixth grade. That he started performing oral sex on me in seventh grade, that sometimes that was all that would happen and other times that would just be the start. That he would ask me if I liked it, and I wouldn't say anything or even look at him; I would just stare at the wall or something behind him, away from him. That he would sometimes say "I love you," and I wouldn't say anything back. That he wouldn't wake me up to initiate sex; I would wake up to him already touching me or on top of me. That he would sometimes tell me to touch his penis, and I would just kind of poke at it. That he would try to put my hand around it, but I would pull away. That he never wore a condom but also never ejaculated inside of me, at least not as far as I knew. That he would always run to the bathroom at the end, and then I'd hear the lock click. When Tommy asked me what I thought Mitch did in the bathroom, I said, "Who knows?" I think I did know that he was masturbating in there to finish himself off, but that part was too hard for me to say.

It was surreal to be saying any of this out loud. Not just because the words were embarrassing, but because they had gone unspoken for so long. Telling Aaron had been weird and difficult enough, and he was someone I loved and trusted. I'd known Tommy for a few hours.

I didn't fully understand at that time that he was just the first of many strangers I'd have to say these embarrassing things to. This was such a new development in something that had been a hidden part of my life for years. Over time, because of repetition and continual analysis, the words would become a little less embarrassing and more matter of fact, but that didn't make them any less painful. Numbness doesn't mean the injury is gone.

"What do you think should happen to your dad?" Tommy asked me.

"I don't know," I said. I truly didn't. The victim Mitch had preyed upon wanted him to waste away in prison, consumed by regret and haunting memories that would make it impossible for him to sleep. His daughter wanted everyone to be back home together and everything to quiet down. Unfortunately, I was both of those people.

"What do you think he's gonna say when I ask him about it?" Tommy asked.

"He'll probably say no." The pit in my stomach dropped farther and wider, like my whole self could collapse down into it. "Or maybe tell the truth. I'm not sure."

Tommy asked what would happen if I told Mitch no. I liked that he asked it that way, rather than asking whether I had tried to tell him no. It implied that he understood it wasn't that simple, that he knew this difficult territory well.

"If I did tell him no, he'd get mad," I said. My voice started letting out the shakiness I always tried so hard to quell; all I could hear in it was weakness. The shakiness was a clear giveaway that I wasn't as in control as I wanted to be and had long been pretending to be. I hated that I couldn't overpower it. "He'd just act mad at me all the time. And I don't really like him mad at me." The last few words were barely audible, little tufts of breath.

The tears I couldn't quite choke back were a new kind I would soon be all too familiar with, a sadness directed equally outward and inward. I was devastated by all that had happened to me and what it meant I had to deal with now; I was also mad at myself for caring how Mitch felt, for denying my own health and happiness for so long because of what he wanted and how he might react. I was embarrassed that I had to give that answer: I didn't like him being mad. The thought of it still made my stomach clench with a familiar dread. If I thought Mitch would have been mad at me before, it was nauseating to think of all I was setting in motion now. I wanted to feel relieved, hopeful, vindicated. Instead, I just felt more and more deflated. I was frustrated by the world and by myself, betrayed by both, disappointed by both.

Then Tommy did something so endearing that it shoved a bit of that pain aside and let in a flicker of comfort. Looking around, he muttered, "Let me get something here" and left the room for a few seconds. He returned with a roll of toilet paper, handing it to me sheepishly. "It's all I got." He gestured toward his face, haltingly. "If you need to...you know." That simple offering represented so much kindness; it resonated for me with an encouraging echo in that void where kindnesses, big or small, had long been lacking. I couldn't help but smile up at him. I even giggled.

As I was getting ready to leave the police station, Tommy said to me, "You'll be safe with me. I can assure you of that." It was the first time in years that I had felt the hope of safety.

All night, as I wrestled with exhaustion, my mind raced, going over my answers and wondering if I'd said enough, if I'd given the detectives what they would need. I felt bad when I had to tell Tommy that I'd taken a shower that morning and that the underwear I'd been wearing the night before was now clean, as Mitch had promptly thrown in a load of laundry. It was so common for him to do laundry when Mom wasn't home that I hadn't seen it as suspicious, hadn't realized he was being careful to eliminate evidence. (I would later learn how frequently rape kits—forensic exams that look for potential evidence of sexual assault—can be inconclusive even when those sorts of tangible things are available.) I wished I could hand Tommy and Wayne solid, physical evidence that they could throw in Mitch's face and make this a done deal. I hoped my words could provide the weapons they would need. If I was going to do this, I wanted to do it right.

It was nearing midnight when I left that draining interview, and still my night was far from over. The detectives requested that I have a rape kit done as soon as possible, so they had an investigator from the Department of Children's Services drive me the forty-five minutes from the station to Nashville General Hospital for a physical and gynecological exam. Mitch's mother, Grandma Sally, rode along with me, which was no comfort; I didn't have a close relationship with her or Grandpa John. We didn't know each other well. I'm sure she was confused and concerned, but Grandma spent much of that night saying there had better not be anything happening that was going to get anyone in trouble or break up the family. It was accusatory. It reminded me of my mother. She knew that the detectives had ordered a rape kit. Surely she knew what that meant. In fact, she used to work in a hospital, so I'm sure she knew all too well. I squirmed in my seat, wishing I could get farther away from her and unsure of what to expect at the hospital.

A few years later, just one week after Mitch's sentencing for his crimes against me, Grandpa John would be arrested for indecent exposure after dropping his pants twice in front of children. There were accusations that it had happened before that, too. While he'd never acted like that around me, I had long known that he had strange interests and habits. He'd lived with us for a while, when we first moved to Tennessee. I can still remember the reverberations of Mom's screaming at him after discovering that he'd been taking tampon applicator tubes out of the bathroom trash and carrying them around in his pockets. In the case of that father-son relationship, the apple definitely did not fall far from the tree.

When we arrived at the hospital, the staff all talked to Grandma instead of me, almost like I wasn't there. I assume that's standard, talking to the adult instead of the minor. The emergency room was chaotic even in those early-morning hours, so many crises clamoring to be addressed at once. I was too numb to ask questions, so I just stood there and waited—waited to be spoken to, or given directions, or given some sense of reassurance. It was all so routine for the hospital staff, going through their steps, while my entire world had been jolted so fiercely that it felt like a miracle I was still standing on my feet.

Soon, I was waiting instead on an exam table in a paper gown that was so thin and awkward it seemed mostly to serve as an inconvenience. My whole body was shaking. I was the kind of numb where you can *feel* that you're numb, can feel your body wanting to shut down. It took concentration to stay awake and relatively calm. It was so tempting to fall asleep right there, to refuse to talk to anyone, or to walk out and leave all of it behind.

But I knew there was no leaving it behind. I knew my fight wasn't over yet. I had to keep going, had to endure these steps to get to the resolution I needed.

It felt so awkward to be naked on that table, to have the nurse practitioner, Lisa, sitting between my legs and looking closely at my vagina. The metal of the speculum was cold and felt so invasive. I fought the urge to close my legs. I had never been to a gynecologist's office, so even the routine stuff was foreign and uncomfortable for me. I didn't even know there *was* routine stuff women had done, or what that would be.

Lisa performed a complete genital and anal exam and looked me over from head to toe, taking samples along the way: strands of my hair, swabs from inside my mouth, and a draw of blood that left a huge bruise on my arm, an embarrassing reminder that lingered for days afterward. She had me pee in a cup for a pregnancy test, which thankfully came back negative and didn't take long to show the result. She explained that the hospital would test my blood for HIV, hepatitis B, and syphilis. I hadn't even considered what would happen if I'd gotten pregnant or contracted a disease. At fifteen. From my dad.

I wished I wasn't in there alone, but then a harsh voice in my head asked me who I'd expect to be there with me, and my loneliness deepened. I wanted my mom there, but my reality was already shifting enough that I knew the reassurance I was longing for wasn't something she could provide. Nana was hundreds of miles away. My friends wouldn't understand what I was dealing with. And it was no comfort to know that Grandma Sally was out in the waiting room, that I'd have to face her again when it was time to leave. She was only another form of examination now, a critical eye looking me over and doubting me.

Lisa went through a list of questions to determine what factors might come into play in collecting evidence. My heart sank a bit as I had to report that, yes, since the last sexual contact, I had showered, consumed food and drink, urinated, defecated, brushed my teeth, used mouthwash, and changed my clothes. Again, I worried I was hurting my case and felt like I was letting people down, including myself. Did she or the detectives tell me then how often these reports come back inconclusive? That it could take a week for us to get the results? And that, if ejaculation had not occurred, there would be nothing there to find and the test would come back negative? I don't remember. If they did, it didn't register. But Lisa would later testify in court, and had noted in her written report from that night, that her exam "neither rules in nor rules out the possibility of sexual contact." The findings of a gynecological exam can be "normal" even if someone has been sexually assaulted.

She gave me a prescription for Plan B, to lower the risk of becoming pregnant from the most recent rape, and some other sort of medication, I think to prevent a sexually transmitted infection. I was suffering from information overload and didn't understand what either medication was for, but I was too afraid and in shock to ask questions. I told her I wanted to wait and talk to my mom about the medications before I started taking them. Lisa tried to explain that Plan B should be taken within seventy-two hours of intercourse, that the sooner I took it, the better chance it had of being effective.

I don't remember that conversation now. It's yet another

thing I learned of (or relearned, I guess) by looking through documentation several years later. I'm sure my ears heard the words as Lisa said them, but my brain couldn't process them and certainly didn't retain them. None of this was real. That sort of denial was something way beyond the sense of infallibility typical of teenagers. I knew I wasn't infallible; I'd had plenty of damage done to me already. But these additional threats lurking, these potential aftereffects of the abuse, were too much for my brain to grasp. My head was in such a fog that it muddled most of what Lisa was trying to say to me. The details of everything that had happened that night were fuzzy before I'd even left the hospital.

I know now that the voice in my head that night was all too right: I shouldn't have been there alone.

Lisa wrote her pager number on the discharge instruction sheet she gave me, so that my mom could contact her once she got home to discuss the medications and next steps. Because of how recently the last sexual contact had occurred, she also recommended repeat testing for pregnancy and infections. "Family is encouraged to call with any questions or concerns," she wrote. You would think there would be *many* questions and concerns. But Lisa would not hear from my mother.

Concerned, Lisa would be the one to call, a few days later. My mother would tell her that we had not discussed the medications and I had not taken them. She would tell her that she had not received the discharge instructions, and Lisa would then mail her a copy.

My mother would *not* tell Lisa that I tried asking her about the medications. That she brushed the topic away like an annoying insect, saying we'd discuss it later. I assume she must have known that this wasn't something that should be delayed—if she had believed there was anything to worry about. She would not tell Lisa that I gave it a day or two and then brought up the topic again. That she told me not to take the pills. That she said I didn't need them. As uncertain as I may have been then about the medications and their implications and what this all might mean, I was already pretty certain that her dismissiveness about the hospital's instructions meant she didn't believe me.

Of course, as I left the hospital that night, I didn't yet know what awaited me upon my mom's return. I believed we would talk about the medications and the countless other ramifications of the abuse, and that we would sort it all out together. I was eager for her to get home and make everything make sense.

I didn't know why Caleb and I stayed at Mitch's parents' apartment that night; I would have rather stayed with friends. I later found out it was what Mitch had decided, after Tommy and Wayne finished interviewing him and told him he'd be going to jail that night. Grandma and I got to their apartment around four or five a.m. Caleb was already there with Grandpa John, and they were both asleep, which was a relief; I didn't want to have to talk to anyone else. After I finally collapsed into bed, Grandma came into the room and told me to give her my phone. I was so used to it in those days that I didn't protest or ask why, but it felt violating and added to my sense that she was not on my side. There was always such an air of distrust, when all I was trying to do was tell the long-hidden truth and get help. Thinking back on it, I have to wonder if keeping my phone away from me was Mitch's suggestion.

II.

The next day, I had to repeat much of the same information to a forensic investigator named Colleen at the Child Advocacy Center (CAC). I didn't know what that was or what would happen when I got there. So much was happening in this twenty-four-hour period that it was all a dizzying blur. Grandma drove me there, amidst more questioning, and said she'd wait for me outside. I later found out that she came in and told some of the staff there that I was a liar and that the alleged abuse didn't happen. (I also later saw in the report from my hospital exam that Grandma expressed "a low level of concern of sexual abuse of Jessica by her son.") Already, I was being sabotaged by people I should have been able to count on, people who should have been assumed to want to protect a child.

Colleen told me that our conversation was being recorded and that the detectives were watching from another room. I felt like I was being studied under a magnifying glass, passed around from one researcher to another.

We started with what felt like small talk, as Colleen worked through some background to get a sense of our family dynamics. At the time, they seemed like trivial questions, and I was a little frustrated, antsy to get on to the much more pressing issues at hand. My answers were short and quiet— my typical demeanor, heightened by the circumstances.

"What's something y'all like to do together?" Colleen asked.

I thought for a moment, first wondering why *that* was what she wanted to know, and then struggling to come up with an example.

"Sometimes we go watch a movie in Nashville together," I answered.

"Anything else?"

"We don't really do much."

"Do you and your mom get along well?" Her voice had a fakeness to it, a lightheartedness that was probably an intentional effort to comfort children. To me, it just felt awkward, like we were staying far on the outskirts of what was real. I started to get the sense that this was just a warm-up act, as we inched closer to the scary stuff.

I nodded and gave an "mmhmm" without hesitation. My sweet naïveté at that age still wanted this to be truer than it was.

"What's something fun you like to do with your mom?" she prodded.

"Shopping," I said with a smile and a little laugh. As if my life with my mother were about simple pleasures like new clothes and food-court lunches.

"What about your dad?"

Ah, now we were getting somewhere, zeroing in on the reason I'd been brought to this beige room.

"Sometimes we go to Go USA with my brother." It was our favorite amusement park, not far from our apartment. We could play in the arcade and ride go-karts like we were a normal family.

"And are you pretty close to him?"

"Kinda, yeah."

Again, I wondered if my answers were okay. I was telling the truth, but was I offering up the right parts of it? Were my examples helpful?

Colleen put some markers and a drawing of a girl's body on the table in front of me. She had me draw an X on the parts I didn't like having touched, then put an X in a different color on the parts where someone had touched me. My two kinds of Xs overlapped in each area.

She asked me who had touched me there.

I said, "My dad."

We went through the same line of questioning as the night before: the wheres and whens and hows. I again had to say that I couldn't remember exactly what he or I had been wearing, much of what he had said, or any particular sounds or smells. Were these tests I was failing? Throughout it all, I was so unsure of what would happen next, of what my answers would mean, of what I might be setting into motion.

The recorded conversation is difficult to watch back. I was a timid little girl. The dissociative state I'd come to know so well allowed a level of detachment between my mind and the words I was saying, so that I could largely report what had happened in a matter-of-fact way, almost robotic at times. Other than the brief use of the markers, I sat the entire time with my arms crossed tight against my chest, my shoulders hunched forward, like I was collapsing in on myself.

I told Colleen that Mitch's advances would often occur in small doses, as he seized any pocket of time he could find. He would come into my room for a minute or two while Mom was busy doing laundry. She and Caleb had both been home many times when Mitch would risk a quick touch of my breasts, if not more.

He had continued his practice of spanking me with my pants and panties down into my teenage years. I remember it happening once when I was in ninth grade, for getting "just" an eighty-eight on a test at school. (My grades had often suffered much worse than that, given the trauma he was putting me through.) Mom was home at that time, but she had such a barricade up about the whole situation that she might as well not have been. And there were several times when we were in Mom and Mitch's bedroom with the door locked, and Caleb would knock, calling for his dad. After rushing to put his pants on, Mitch would open the door, and I would come walking out seconds later, not sure how I was supposed to act.

I relived more of the specifics for Colleen, most of which thankfully no longer take up residence in my memory but which I have watched my past self recount on the recorded interview: The first time it happened was in my bed, at night when I had been sleeping. I remembered waking up, on my back, with him lying on top of me. He had his pants down. I had my pajamas on, but he had pulled my pants down a bit and was trying to insert himself. Eventually, he did. He kept getting up to check to make sure my mom wasn't awake, and then he would come back and do it again.

I told her I wasn't sure when the next time was.

"It wasn't as frequent back then as it is now, since I want to go hang out with my friends more often now, and that's when it happens," I said. I was still using the present tense. I wasn't yet looking at this as something that was over. I couldn't yet pack it away as something from my past.

"And why did you wait so long to tell?" The soft Southern drawl of her voice padded this question with understanding.

"I just...didn't want to really talk about it." My voice kept dropping out every few syllables as I fought to keep the emotion pushed to the back of my throat.

Colleen gave a lot of okays and all rights, like soothing a baby. She asked me what I would think about while the abuse was going on.

"I would just stare at the wall," I croaked out in a hoarse whisper, "and wish that he's not doing that."

Colleen asked me to tell her how I felt about what had happened between Mitch and me. That question made me a little angry. How did she *think* I felt? And how could I possibly put those feelings into words?

"I mean, I don't like it, but...he's my dad," I said. Some tears escaped with that answer.

At the time, and for the several years beforehand, that seemingly simple fact, *He's my dad*, had meant, *What could I do? What choice do I have?* An acquiescence. But now, it makes me furious; it means he took advantage of a position of power and left me feeling unable to question it. It also means that I loved him and wanted to trust him, which makes me sad about the situation both then and now.

"It was scary at first," I added, "but I've gotten used to it."

That statement of defeat was what had defined my life for more than four years.

After I told her that we'd stayed with Mitch's parents the night before, Colleen asked, "And have you been able to talk to your grandparents about any of this?"

"No," I said, the pitch of my voice getting higher. "I don't really want to."

"What makes it hard to talk to them about this?"

"I'm just not very close to them." I shook my head, blinking frantically, wishing it all away.

Those questions blared a spotlight on how deeply alone I was feeling, unable to talk to the people I was sent to stay with by my rapist the night I reported his years of abuse. Nana and Poppy were the ones I wanted there. My chest was heavy with the wish for them to know the truth.

They had long been uncomfortable with Mitch's presence in my life and distrusting of both him and my mother. Nana had tried so many times over the years to make her concerns clear to her daughter, but Mom, ever the master of manipulation, would always somehow change the subject, avoid the conversation entirely, or simply get angry and drive a further wedge in their relationship. If she wasn't speaking to Nana, she couldn't hear the things she didn't want to hear.

Nana had sometimes tried, delicately, to broach the subject with me, too. I remember a day when I was maybe fourteen years old and Nana took me shopping. She pointed out some cute shorts she thought I might like. She had good taste; they were cuffed extra short, with some distressed detail, and would have looked great on me. But just looking at them gave me a queasy feeling.

"Mitch wouldn't let me wear those," I said. "Maybe around the house, but not out in public."

"Why does Mitch choose your clothes, instead of your mom?" she asked.

"Mom just goes along with whatever Mitch says," I told her.

Just as I had done for so many years. Just as I had been conditioned to do.

And now I was alone, in the third unfamiliar room I'd been ushered to in less than twenty-four hours, speaking my truth to yet another stranger, whose questions seemed to be operating on autopilot. To Colleen, this was a job, these were standard questions; she had clearly been through them all many times before. But this was my life on display, my secrets and shame and trauma. Nana and Poppy were far away and didn't yet know all that had come to light and all that was crumbling down around me. The grandparents I was staying with might as well have been the ones who were hundreds of miles away, given the emotional void that lay between us.

All of that came out in those tears. The fight was just beginning, and I didn't know who, if anyone, would be in my corner.

III.

While I was at the CAC, my mom was on her way home from the airport, having just returned from two long days of traveling back from Africa. I had been telling Aaron—and reminding myself—for days that I would tell my mom about the abuse once she got home. By this point, though, I knew she must have talked to Mitch, at least within the last few hours, now that she was back in the country and could be reached on her cell phone. I felt oddly removed from it all, logistically; I wasn't sure who was talking to whom, what they were saying or believing. I didn't know how soon I would see Mom, or what she would have heard by the time I did.

I certainly didn't expect the reception I got. Maybe I should have. But the young girl in me hoped the opening of this box of awful secrets would allow me to turn to my mother for comfort, that it would activate the nurturing role I hadn't often seen in her. As afraid as I had been to let the truth come out, there was some sort of anticipated relief now that it *was* out; I was a new kind of afraid now, and I was ready to seek her help in dealing with it all.

Grandma Sally brought me back to the police station and into the same interview room I'd been in the night before, where my mother had just finished talking with the detectives and was waiting to see me. I knew Tommy and Wayne wanted Mom and me to have the opportunity to see each other, assuming we'd have a lot to sort out and a lot of emotions to work through. But it seemed Mom wanted to see me to interrogate me. Her questions were more critically crafted than those of the people responsible for working the case.

When I walked into the room, Mom just blinked at me. There was no smile, no hug, no look of relief to see me alive

61

and safe. There were no tears. For probably a full thirty seconds or more, we said nothing to each other—an eternity, given all there was to be said. This was the first time we had seen or had the chance to speak to each other in two weeks.

Again, I sat with my arms crossed tight, hunched over, looking alternately at my mother and at the table between us. Watching that tape back, I can see that my body language conveyed the pain I was feeling. Mom sat with her hands folded on top of the table, carefully poised. We were like actors portraying a cold, distant relationship, formal at best.

Finally, she spoke. "So, all of this is true?"

I nodded.

"And when did it begin?" she asked.

"Sixth grade," I said in a little squeak of a whisper.

And then, immediately, she tightened the screws of the mental vise she was all too prepared to put me in.

"You understand what happens from here, right?" she said. "You understand that, if you're telling the truth, your dad will be going to prison. He will be there for a long time."

She was looking for me to crack, to say I'd made it all up.

I reminded myself that she had been traveling for close to twenty-four hours, probably with little sleep, and that she must be overwhelmed to come home to these developments. But we were all tired and reeling. And I really thought she had suspected that something was going on all along.

In a disorienting shift, she added that if I was saying this really was the truth, she would have to believe me. She repeated it twice, like she was reminding herself: "...then I have to believe you. I have to believe you." Her voice got higher in pitch on the second one. She sounded a little desperate. But she wasn't ready to believe.

She asked me again when it began, and then how.

I started crying and was instantly mad at myself for doing

so. Mom had always told me that crying was a sign of weakness. I tried not to let her ever see me vulnerable like that.

I told her it had started in my room, at night, when she was asleep.

She seemed not to be able to comprehend this, because Grandpa John had been staying with us at the time. Mom asked about him sleeping on the couch, I guess thinking that he would have seen or heard something. I wanted to tell her that it didn't matter who was around, that she had been right there next to us more times than I could count, and Mitch would watch her carefully while he laid me over the edge of the bed. At some point I did acknowledge that it had happened in their room, too. She seemed increasingly flustered at times, but more confused or irritated than concerned. Not once did she express concern or regret or anger at Mitch.

She asked if he would put anything on his penis, and where he would go to masturbate. That question made no sense to me, and I know Tommy was hung up on it later and tried to get clarification from her, with no luck. Was that Mitch's typical way of finishing things off after sex? Or did she suspect something about it because she knew more than she was willing to let on?

Despite those initial tears, I generally maintained my composure well and answered her questions readily, giving the same sorts of answers I'd already had to give the detectives and the CAC investigator. Clearly not satisfied with the direction things were taking, Mom changed tactics.

"So, your dad caught you and Aaron on the couch?" she said. "Why did he have to take him home? He caught him lying on top of you." The last part was a statement, not a question. She and Mitch had clearly discussed this, and already the argument that would become the basis of his defense was taking shape. Already they were shaming the victim and trying to get me to back down out of embarrassment.

"Were you guys kissing?" she continued. "You were upset that Dad was gonna be disappointed in you."

"For what? For kissing him? No," I retorted, in a rare burst of audible irritation.

Mom sighed and shifted in her seat, like she was getting exasperated and trying to keep her composure. She asked me how many times it had happened. I almost had to scoff, realizing just how adamantly blind she was being to the reality of the situation. Did she think this was some passing fluke that had happened once or twice? I had already told her that we were talking about *years* of abuse. I couldn't have kept track of a total number if I'd wanted to. It was ever-present in my day-to-day life, either the abuse itself or the threat of it happening at any moment.

I told her I hadn't kept count, but that it would happen whenever I wanted to go see someone.

"So you did it several times, then," she said.

Her use of "you" there was frustrating—and, again, indicative of a pattern to come—because it felt accusatory, making it seem like a mutual act between Mitch and me, with shared responsibility. This was not something *we* did; it was something—many things—done *to me*. I was without action in it all, and without a voice.

"I'm having a hard time absorbing this, as you would know," Mom said. "Part of me wants to believe you, and then a part of me is like, 'This cannot be happening.'"

It was the most logical she'd sounded yet. In that moment, she was almost compassionate. She was human. And she was right that I would know that overwhelming, surreal feeling. I'd been going through a similar cycle of disbelief myself for years.

But then she was cracking her knuckles—whether a nervous tic or an attempt to look tough, I'm not sure—and saying that we wouldn't be able to go home, that she didn't know whether we would stay nearby or go back to New York.

Throughout all of this, I said very little. I felt like there wasn't much more I *could* say, if Mom wasn't yet accepting the main concept around which everything else revolved.

She would continue to flip-flop a couple more times, trying out every tactic to see what would land. Trying to follow along was like a nauseating agility test.

Next it was, "Know that no matter what, if it's not the truth or [if it is] the truth, that I will love you, and our family will work through this, with or without your father."

That was merely an elaborate preface to the fact that she wanted to ask me one more time, before she'd open the door to call Tommy and Wayne back in, if I was "sure" I was telling the truth. She actually used the words "the whole truth and nothing but the truth," making me feel all the more like I was already testifying on the witness stand.

"Understand that I love you and would not be angry with you," she added.

I wanted so badly to believe that. It was the kind of thing I needed to hear, but not just as empty words. She seemed angry already, there in that room, her anger a haze that loomed around us. Fear clawed at my throat and obscured my voice—fear of her and that anger, fear of disappointing her or hurting her, fear of all that was already unfolding and falling down around us. All I could do was continue to nod and say through my sniffling that, yes, it was the truth, while I silently berated myself for crying.

Suddenly, in the most blindsiding shift of all, she wanted to know, "Did you ever bleed afterwards?" Clearly this had just popped into her head as an opportunity to trip me up, a piece of evidence I couldn't provide.

I was somewhat annoyed, maybe even a little embarrassed, that I had to say no. I would come to learn later that many young women's hymens are broken from intense physical activity like dance or cheerleading, both of which I had long been a part of, or even from riding a bike. It had likely happened for me years earlier, without my even knowing. But I'm sure Mom considered it a small victory—as the defense team certainly did later—that this was not something damning that could be used against Mitch.

Mom started to get up from the table but then tossed out one last scare tactic, saying she didn't know if they were going to arrest my dad, or what would happen next. I didn't know either, of course, but her attempt to throw that heavy dash of guilt at me didn't sway me. I was already so thoroughly in the tumult that all I could do was keep tumbling and see where I wound up, hoping that the end result would be less dizzying than the past four years had been.

I was running on maybe two hours of sleep, which had been sandwiched between the trip to the hospital in Nashville and hours of questioning at the CAC and now the police station again. And it was the kind of incomplete, disorienting sleep you get in an unfamiliar place; I kept waking up unsure of where I was, which added to the blur of all that had unfolded and all that was to come. So, by now, I was feeling pretty numb. Maybe, I considered fleetingly, I was actually still asleep, in my own bed at home, and none of this was really happening.

If it *was* happening, I kept thinking there would be signs of comfort, of a turning point reached at last. The feeling of uneasiness that persisted, the sense that my mother was not hearing anything I was saying, was very much like a night-mare I couldn't pull myself out of.

If Nana and Poppy had been there, the first thing they would have done was hug me and ask if I was okay.

Mom's last words to me before she opened the door were, "So, that's it? You're sticking to it?"

I nodded. She opened the door, and I walked out, feeling like I was taking the first step onto an unknown planet. My feet felt clumsy and awkward, as if my legs had fallen asleep. All of the weight that had started to lift off my shoulders in reporting the abuse had now come straight back, pressing down on me.

Throughout our conversation, it had become clear—painfully clear, in the most literal sense—that an irreversible shift was happening. I had worried that speaking up about the abuse would tear my family apart. But I hadn't antici-pated that it would tear my family away *from me*, that it would turn my mother against me. I had worried only about Mitch being taken away and the emotional repercussions that would bring for the three of us, at home without him. I could see now that a different kind of separation was taking place.

My mother didn't believe me. She didn't want to. She would choose not to.

A policewoman I crossed paths with in the hallway said, "I saw your mom didn't give you a hug. So, I will."

Wrapped awkwardly in this kind woman's arms, I felt both comfort and a crushing sadness. I was like an animal at a shelter, looking for someone to take it in.

Watching Others Speak

There are many aspects of the investigation that I didn't know about until years later, even after the trial, since many of the detectives' recorded interviews that were not admitted in court were later obtained by Nana and Poppy. They provide critical background to some of what unfolded, even though I first encountered them after the fact. It is such a bizarre, disorienting experience to see behind closed doors and hear conversations about me and about events that would come to determine so much of the course of my life.

One of those conversations is Mitch's initial interview with Tommy and Wayne at the police station, which would have been about an hour after they'd interviewed me. When first explaining to Mitch that they were taking me to the station to talk further, I learned later, Wayne had recommended that Mitch get himself over there soon as well. Upon first playing the video, I was startled to see Caleb sitting across the table from him. It made sense, I guess; he was too young to be left home alone. But that poor kid had no idea of the reality dictating their current situation, no idea what he was sitting just on the outskirts of. If he knew the details—the *truth*—as to why his dad had been told to go there and wait in that dingy room, maybe he would have seen that he was sitting across from a monster.

I don't think it's just my interpretation that the air of that little room was thick with tension; I could feel it prickling along my skin while watching the recording. As Mitch waited for the detectives to come in, he joked around and made small talk with Caleb, trying to give off a relaxed, carefree air, pretending everything was fine. But all the while he was wringing his hands, sighing, and shifting around in his chair, and he kept moving his keys on the table from one spot to another, as if looking to feel settled. They made him wait a long time.

Caleb grabbed the toilet paper that was still sitting on the table and started tossing it back and forth between his hands, letting it roll around playfully, mindlessly, like any bored child might, needing something to busy his hands with. He couldn't have known, of course, that it was there because it had been offered to me less than an hour before in an attempt to dry the tears caused by the predator who now sat across from him. That Tommy had offered me whatever he could to try to console me and, through that simple, humble action, had made me feel more protected than I had in my own home for years. He couldn't have known that what he so carelessly tossed between his small hands was a symbol of the pain his father had caused me, the pain he was currently waiting to answer for.

"I wonder what this is all about," Caleb said softly. He kept resting his chin on his arms, folded on the table.

Mitch said nothing. I can only imagine the responses that went through his head.

Caleb asked if he would have to go away for the night, to

stay with Mom's friend who sometimes looked after us. His voice was full of the irritated dread that preteens can slip into so easily.

"Probably. I don't know yet," Mitch answered curtly.

"I don't know why. I didn't do nothing," Caleb said, his confusion heavy with irritation.

"You didn't do anything," Mitch agreed. I watched it back multiple times to analyze how much of an emphasis he placed on the word *you*.

Tommy called Caleb out of the room before starting the interview. And then Mitch waited, alone, for several more minutes.

As soon as the detectives sat down, Mitch slid his keys across the table, toward the corner where Wayne was sitting. Wayne picked them up and turned them over in his hands, his brow furrowed, as if trying to decode a mysterious object. Mitch detailed where his car was parked.

"Well, that's *your* keys," Wayne said, handing them back.

"I know," Mitch faltered. "That's why I got 'em sitting there."

Throughout their twenty-minute conversation, Mitch only once attempted to deny the allegations. After Wayne told him what they had heard and mentioned that I'd said Mitch had had sex with me the night before, Mitch replied, "That's not accurate. No, I did not have sex with her." This must have been an issue of semantics, a technicality, as a way of evading the truth; either he didn't qualify whatever actions he'd taken that night as "sex" or he was confusing the timing of it. It is not the answer of someone who's innocent. It is not the answer of someone who's truly confused or shocked by an accusation.

Aside from that one comment, throughout the rest of the conversation, Mitch's only form of denying what he'd done was to awkwardly avoid answering questions at all. Poor Wayne—who, I think, didn't want to believe what was happening, having thought he knew Mitch as a good person—asked Mitch so many times, in so many ways, trying to give him the opportunity to say he was innocent.

"She says this has been going on for quite a while," Wayne said. "Would you care to comment on that?"

"Um, no, I wouldn't care to comment on that either," Mitch said.

His awkward non-answers continued throughout the conversation: "I'm trying to understand why everything has come to be." "I don't know what I'm supposed to do here." "I don't know what to say." "I guess there's nothing more to discuss."

Wayne asked him outright if I was lying.

"At this point, I don't even know how to answer your question," said Mitch.

"Is it true?" Wayne pressed. His frustration was showing through under the cool demeanor he'd tried to maintain, his voice rising there nearly to a shout. There was a sort of laugh to it, too; one of thorough astonishment.

"I've got nothing more to say," Mitch said. "If she says it's true, then that's what it is. It is what it is."

That's a confession. It still makes my jaw clench that this interview was not admitted in court. The defense team filed a motion to have it suppressed, and a judge granted it, because Mitch's answers were "ambiguous."

Wayne said this should be an easy answer, and yet clearly Mitch couldn't say it. Mitch said nothing in response. Wayne acknowledged that maybe this was just too big a topic for Mitch to be ready to talk about. Still, he said nothing.

Since Mitch was clearly getting anxious, they all agreed

to wait until he got an attorney before discussing things further. He was afraid of saying too much.

Wayne told Mitch right then and there that he had heard all he needed to hear, and that he believed the allegations were true based on Mitch's demeanor. And he told him that they couldn't let him go home that night; he'd be under arrest and have to stay the night in jail.

I didn't know where he had gone that night. I didn't see him again from the moment the cops knocked on the door until our first day in the courtroom.

Another recorded conversation I gained access to long after the fact is the one my mother had with Tommy and Wayne just before they'd brought me into the room to talk to her. It's interesting to see how much, at that early point, she claimed she wasn't sure what to believe and rather defensively said she wasn't trying to take sides. It's also interesting to see how much those claims were interwoven with dismissive descriptions of me as a liar. She acted as if she had no choice but to question thoroughly the things I had said about Mitch, based on examples as long-ago and trivial as stupid fibs I had told in elementary school.

When Wayne started the conversation by saying he wasn't taking anyone's side, that he just wanted to know if something had happened to me, Mom *said* she agreed. But just seconds later, within the first minute of their conversation, she was saying, "Jessica lies a *lot*." She emphasized how often she had talked with her friends about this alleged pattern of mine, as if prepared to hand over evidence against me. How could she be so ready to disprove me before even seeing or speaking to me? "Sometimes I have to ask her over and over before finally she breaks," she told them. And that's exactly what she tried to do during our conversation there: break me.

Wayne and Tommy came to my defense by saying that if this was a lie, it was a very detailed one, stretching back over several years. "That's a lot to maintain," Wayne told her. They were well versed in liars, and often the inconsistencies in the stories would give them away. Tommy said I remembered a lot of details that a typical liar, especially at fifteen years old, would not. The details of my story were consistent, they seemed to be telling her, because they were facts.

Mom said if it was proven that Mitch had done something to me, their relationship would be over. Here, *she* was clearly the liar, as she later entered the courtroom as part of Mitch's defense team, and no amount of evidence or debate would sway her.

She talked about God a lot, as she would continue to do in the years ahead, saying she had been "without ceasing in prayer," for the truth to be revealed and for me to find deliverance from a lying tongue. As their interview ended, Wayne asked Mom if there was anything he could do. She said, "Just pray that the truth will be revealed, either way." I guess she just kept waiting for God to say what she wanted Him to say.

Tommy and Wayne told Mom in great detail just how terribly their interview with Mitch had gone, that the things he had said (and not said) to them—failing to deny the accusations, refusing to call me a liar—led them to believe *he* had been the one lying to her.

Wayne said he'd heard Mitch was complaining about them not believing him. "There's nothing for me to believe, because he didn't deny it!" Wayne told her, in a tone still so shocked that it practically came out as a laugh. "He has not made a denial, at all!"

73

They also told Mom how they'd emphasized to me that if there was any part of what I'd told them that wasn't true, they needed to end it now—that this would be the time, before things got too out of hand. They were giving me an out, in case I'd gotten carried away and said things I couldn't stand behind. But I didn't need that out. I only needed for this long-hidden truth to finally make things change for the better.

They offered to let Mom watch the tape of their interview with Mitch—something Wayne said he had never offered anyone in his twenty-year career. At first, Mom said she wasn't ready to watch it; she needed time—but, as far as I know, she continued to turn down the opportunity every time it was offered. Had she watched it, I don't think she could have believed he was innocent. And I think she knew that. In fact, Wayne had told her outright that he thought it would convince her of Mitch's guilt. He said he was confident that between that interview and my statement, Mitch would go to prison. So she made a deliberate choice to believe—to pretend to believe—the less inconvenient version of things, one where she could try to keep a husband at the expense of a daughter.

Not long after that, within a month of the report, Mitch took a bunch of sleeping pills. I don't know if he was just trying to lull himself into a night of uninterrupted sleep or if he was hoping never to wake up. But when Grandma Sally found him, breathing but lethargic, she was concerned enough that she called 911. Grandpa John can be heard in the background of the recorded call, saying, "Come on, buddy," trying to coax Mitch into standing up.

I was out with Mom when she got the call about it. A

74

proud but nervous holder of a learner's permit, I was practicing my driving. I didn't know who had called or what they were saying, but suddenly, frantically, Mom shrieked at me to pull over. She sounded like the air was being ripped out of her lungs. I fumbled for the turn signal and tried to check my mirrors as I careened toward the curb. Mom flung her door open and went running out. Two of my friends were in the backseat and near tears from the sudden fright of it all. We weren't far from the apartment, thankfully. I don't remember how we got the rest of the way there.

Like a flash-forward on a TV show, my next memory of that day is Mom coming home from the hospital, late, bleary-eyed, saying Mitch was on life support and probably wasn't going to make it.

What a thing to say to a child. Especially when it's a lie. He was never on life support. They kept him in the hospital for a few days, and then he got out and carried on with his life.

Mom later told Nana that when she went to see Mitch in the hospital, she asked him, "Did you do this to my daughter?" I have to interpret this to mean that even she could see then that his actions didn't exactly declare innocence.

According to Mom, Mitch's response was to ask God to take him home to Heaven right then if he were guilty.

So, Mom felt she got her answer, the one she'd been waiting for and praying for, when she went back to the hospital the next day and Mitch was still alive. She had heard from God what she'd wanted to hear.

———

In February, four months after the report and the initial series of conversations at the police station, Mom met with Tommy again for another recorded interview. She brought her attorney with her. This recording documents several frustrating things.

First, she lied to Tommy about some of her past drama with Nana and Poppy. She brought up the grandparents' rights they had sued for just before we'd moved to Tennessee, telling Tommy that the request pertained only to me, not to Caleb, and that the judge had denied it because (in my mother's words) Nana "wasn't being fair." In truth, they had pursued rights for visitation with both of us and were granted them.

This is the kind of deceit I was up against throughout my battle for justice. It's so maddening to try to refute someone who continually spouts lies so smoothly, so effortlessly, that I could never even wrap my head around it. I still can't. And it's all the more maddening when that person is your own family. Just as adamantly as I would state, over and over again, what had happened to me—every painful detail of where and when and how—Mitch and my mother and their team would insist on an alternate reality. To rattle off lies like that one about the grandparents' rights, which are proven incorrect in public documentation, goes beyond any level of potential misunderstanding or innocent ignorance. She *had* to have known that she was wrong, had to have been deliberately ignoring the truth and fabricating her own. How could she stomach it? How could she carry that in her conscience? How can she still today?

Second, Mom told Tommy that the icy reception I'd gotten from her in that room months before, when the topic of the abuse sat between us openly for the first time, was purely a product of her jet lag and exhaustion, a moment of weakness that had since been corrected.

"What you seen that night is not the way that my home is

76

at this time," she told him. "She is being supported, she is being loved, she is being taken care of, she is being provided for."

She gave him an example about having taken me to Walmart to buy candy molds so we could make chocolates for Valentine's Day. This is a tough one for me. I remember that day fondly. It was one of a long stretch of in-between days, when Mom was in and out of my life. There were days, like that one, that gave me a sense that things could still be normal, days when she would call me and say, "Mommy's on her way home," or would chat with me in the evenings like I was her friend. While we went to Walmart that day, browsing through trays of tiny heart shapes, the aisles an explosion of red and pink, Mitch was having one of his scheduled visits with Caleb at our apartment. That meant, of course, that I needed to leave. Being able to do something fun with that window of time, something that a mother-daughter duo without a massive family secret imploding between them might do, was such a comfort. It made me feel like Mom cared about me and valued her time with me—and, even now, I wonder if maybe she really did. We'd had a disadvantage from the start; because Mom had gotten pregnant with me when she was so young, we'd never bonded very closely. There had been a disconnect between us long before the abuse worked its way into the equation. But she did try. There were moments, at least, that she tried. I still hold those little things close, like chatting and laughing together as we melted the chocolate in the kitchen that night and poured it into the trays. Those were the moments that made me think things might be okay between us, to cling onto the hope that she might believe me at some point. Still today, I'm holding onto that hope, still waiting and wondering if one day, suddenly, finally, she might open her eyes and realize—or be willing to admit—all that really had been happening right in front of her face.

Lastly, though, at the end of that interview, Tommy asked Mom, "Do you have any questions for me at all?"

Her response was simply a "no," tight-lipped and dismissive. She seemed angry with him. Annoyed.

I couldn't help but notice, as I thought over the entirety of the recorded interviews, that everyone else the detectives had talked to—even Aaron's mother, who accompanied him for part of one—had all asked questions and had shown more concern for me and for the steps that lay ahead than my own mother did.

A Black Hole

A LONG FOUR YEARS STRETCHED BETWEEN MITCH'S initial arrest and his conviction, during which my tenuous relationships with my mom and brother were tested, twisted, and snapped. I thought I'd already walked through hell, but this new chapter we'd entered, each of us with such conflicting perspectives and priorities, was an entirely new level of scary. My attorney and my counselor both would later tell me that they'd never seen anything like it—and they'd seen a *lot*. Rather than rallying around me in my greatest time of need, Mom and Caleb chose to turn away from me as if *I* were the criminal, the dangerous one. I was the one they didn't trust. They abandoned me in slow motion.

While the investigation was first going on, I remained at home and somehow coexisted with the two of them. Mitch had made bond pretty quickly, so he was out of jail and staying with his parents, in the apartment complex just across the street. It was like a sick joke; he could hardly have been closer. He might as well have stayed in the garage. I was always viscerally aware of how nearby he was, skittish at the thought of crossing paths with him. This was nothing remotely close to the refuge Tommy and Wayne had emphasized I would need.

The initial plan had been for Mitch to stay at home and for the rest of us to leave. The first night Mom was back in town from Africa, we stayed at her friend's house—the third bed I'd slept in in as many nights—and were planning to be there for the foreseeable future. Tommy quickly recommended that Caleb and I not be uprooted from our familiar surroundings and routine, and that Mitch should be the one to stay elsewhere. I could have gone either way, really; living somewhere else temporarily would have been disorienting, but home was filled with memories of the abuse.

Maybe the only reason I survived the awkward tension of living with family who were continually doubting me was that they routinely left me alone while they went to visit Mitch. We didn't stay cooped up together within the same narrow walls very often. At the same time, that isolation amplified how alone I was through the entire process. Sitting by myself in an empty kitchen, ears ringing, while I knew the three of them were having dinner together, was a gut-punch of a symbol for how stacked the deck was against me. This was the same table where my brother and I used to talk about how our days went, where Mitch would help me with my homework. Thinking back to those days now is like watching movies of someone else's memories.

One day after school, I brought home a photography collage I'd made for art class and showed it to my mom. It was large—twenty by twenty-four, I think—and full of vibrant colors, images of flowers and water attempting to convey a sense of peace. I couldn't help but feel a little surge of pride when Mom took the time to look at it with interest.

"Oh," she said, studying it up and down, "I've never seen that before."

My little surge was swatted away.

"I've been working on this at home for weeks," I said.

The bright reds and pinks now seemed glaring in how harshly they highlighted Mom's absence across those recent months. If she had been around even a little bit, she would have known this was something I'd been investing a lot of time and effort in. But she was detaching herself from everything about me, down to the little day-to-day details like school projects.

My perspective at that time was limited by how young I was and how small the bubble was that contained my entire world. I see things very differently now; I understand them on a level I wasn't capable of back then. Sure, I was aware of being alone a lot. I missed my mom and Caleb when they weren't around. I sometimes felt hungry. I often felt scared, both of what had happened with Mitch and of what was still unfolding in its wake. But the thing I knew best was denial.

I was not raised in a family that talked about mental health. Emotions in general were tricky territory, especially the negative ones. Best to gloss over them or brush them aside. There was no breaking down and crying. If I was sad about a fight with a friend or a junior-high boyfriend breaking up with me, Mitch would tell me I had thirty seconds to cry. After that, you put yourself together and go about your day. There was no such thing as closing myself off in my room to sob for hours and then sulking the rest of the day. If you ignore it, everything is fine.

So, by the time we reached this terrible transition period after the abuse was reported, I was accustomed to telling everyone, including myself, that I was okay. I *had* to be okay. It was such an ingrained way of thinking that I couldn't even see that it was pretend. I didn't realize, *I'm depressed. I'm really* not *okay. What's going on here isn't okay.*

Through my adult eyes, I can see that my mom took the investigation as an opportunity to release herself from her parental responsibilities for me. In fact, it was like she relished punishing me by leaving me wanting. Maybe she was punishing me because she felt powerless to punish Mitch. She had to take her anger out somewhere.

Taking a teenager's cell phone away is, I'm sure, a common form of punishment—but my mother took mine away for a *year*, beginning when Mitch first got arrested. She claimed it wasn't a punishment but was somehow for my safety—then continually left me home alone with no means of contact, as we didn't have a home phone either. Sometimes, she would also take away my key to the apartment, leaving me sitting out front to wait for her for long stretches of time, sometimes hours. Same with the days she was supposed to pick me up from school. I'd be waiting there long after all the other students had left; it was just me, a few teachers working late, and the janitors starting their after-hours routine. I was grateful there were so few people around to notice my embarrassment. I was always the last one left standing outside, waiting, checking the time every few minutes as an entire hour ticked by. I never knew when, or if, she was going to show up.

Not having my own phone meant that my conversations were very carefully limited and monitored—which, of course, was largely the point. Any time I talked to Nana and Poppy, it was on Mom's phone, with her sitting right next to me, so I couldn't say any of the things I really wanted to say or *should* have said. They would ask how I was doing and what was new, and I would give a rush of desperately honest answers in my head but answer out loud with vague simplicities: "Fine." "Not much."

Any time they seemed to sense that I was feeling down, I would try to affect a more upbeat tone or change the subject, so that Mom wouldn't get suspicious and get mad. My grandparents' instincts were more accurate than my own—wiser, hardened. I may have been fooling myself, but I wasn't fooling them.

"Why don't you have your mom get you a new phone, and Nana will pay for it," Nana cooed in my ear on more than one of those calls.

I inserted a canned response: "Thank you, but it's no problem," or "We're getting mine fixed" (even though I knew it would continue to sit hidden away somewhere, fully functional but abandoned, for months more). There were always excuses. I knew what I was expected to say. My mother would come up with anything to try to shoo away questions and prolong the isolation she was forcing on me. Anything to try to get me to break and change my story about Mitch. Change the truth.

The kitchen in those days wasn't just void of company, but of the basic necessities. I couldn't remember the last time Mom had cooked a meal for me. Still, I told myself that was fine. I could pick and scrounge. I could skip a meal and not care. In school, lunchtime was always more about gabbing with my friends than eating, anyway. I tried to make eggs for myself one morning and burned them so badly I had to throw them away. I didn't know what I was doing; it was like suddenly I was expected to be an independent adult, but I'd had no introduction to those kinds of responsibilities.

Again, now that I *am* an adult, this is hard for me to fathom. If I were a mother, I would never leave my kids with so little. Now, I know it was wrong; back then, it was all I knew. Now, I know it wasn't enough. I couldn't see it then—literally could not allow it to be seen or processed. Blinders up. *I'm fine, I'm fine, I'm fine.*

I was also in need of new clothes, growing out of everything I owned. Mom paid no attention, and when I tried to be assertive and ask for them, she dismissed it by saying we didn't have the money. My pants all became a little too short and yet were a little too long to pass as capris; shirt sleeve hems rode up no matter how much I tried to stretch them out longer. I wore the same few pieces over and over again, hoping no one would notice as long as I mixed and matched enough and waited a few days between repeats. I was glad tight-fitting clothes were in fashion and that dance and cheerleading kept me in good shape, so that hopefully my classmates would think I was intentionally choosing such snug fits. In truth, though, I wished I could burrow deep into baggy sweatshirts that would hide my body, my thoughts, my past—everything. I didn't want my body on display. I wanted to disappear.

My body continued to react to the trauma and to the new forms of stress now being added. My face broke out in a rash, and my entire back was covered with acne. My hair was falling out so much that I could run my fingers through it and pull out clumps of it. My back and my hips hurt as if I were decades older and weakened by arthritis. I had headaches all the time. I eventually stopped complaining to my mom about them because she never did anything to help. Sometimes when I was home alone, I would scrounge around, looking for a pain reliever, but the most I ever came across was a bottle of Advil with just a few broken pieces rattling around the bottom. I always felt so stuck in place, unsure of where to turn. Should I ask a friend's parents for a ride to the store?

Did I have enough cash lying around to buy my own pain meds? How much does Advil cost?

I had to wait a month to get my broken glasses fixed. I had to wait a week to get medicine for pink eye. I was always waiting, hoping for a turning point I was pretty sure would never come.

Because my mother saw this draining new reality we'd all been thrust into as something *I* had done, I guess she felt I didn't deserve to be cared for. Maybe she thought I'd surrender and say I had made it all up.

I was being punished for telling the truth—the thing they all kept asking me for, praying for, yet refusing to hear.

Shortly after she'd gotten back from her mission trip, Mom took me to a gynecologist's office up in Nashville, a discreet forty minutes from home, looking to confirm or deny (hoping to deny, I'm sure) what I said had been done to me. This was only a couple days after I'd already endured a complete exam at the hospital that first night of the investigation. But Mom hadn't been there with me, and we hadn't yet gotten any results back; it seemed she wanted to take matters into her own hands and get answers. I was now lying on a harshly lit exam table, my feet in cold stirrups, for the second time that week.

Mom told the nurse practitioner, Sara, that Mitch had been accused of touching me. Her word choices were little knives. "Been accused of"—indicating that she still saw it as merely an accusation, not a horrifying truth. And "touching" me—refusing to acknowledge that we were talking about many more and greater offenses. She told Sara she'd brought me there to determine whether or not I was a virgin.

Sara had Mom leave the room while she examined me. She was gentle and professional, of course, but I hated even touching my own body to shower, let alone having anyone else involved. I lay there, tense and empty, studying the beige ceiling tiles while I waited for it to be over.

Just like I had always done with Mitch.

I was unaware at the time, but Sara would later testify about how unusual my demeanor was, compared to most young patients she'd seen. It stood out to her that I didn't flinch, didn't push back on the stirrups, didn't giggle nervously, didn't get teary-eyed. "I told her what I was going to do and she was totally cooperative," she would testify, remembering me nearly four years later. "She was very stoic about the whole thing. She didn't offer any kind of resistance whatsoever."

My mind may have been racing at the time, but I was good at making it go blank. It took little effort, after all that practice. Just as I'd counted the swirls in the bedroom mirror to detach myself from what Mitch was doing to my body, my eyes traced the thin metal borders of the ceiling tiles while Sara went through her exam, allowing my mind to retreat into their simple maze.

Finally, Sara told me I could sit up. I pulled down the scratchy paper gown to cover as much of my lap as possible and smoothed its creases over and over. I wanted to cover up everything, from my face to my toes. I wanted to bury myself away somewhere where there wouldn't be any more eyes or hands or probes on me.

Sara called my mom back into the room and, to my relief, told her that my body did in fact show signs of the kinds of trauma I had described, and that it had been going on for quite a while. The ease with which she was able to examine me with the speculum indicated numerous acts of sexual intercourse, she said, whereas for a virgin the entrance would be tighter.

I felt a surge of gratitude toward her, and a sort of smug

satisfaction. *There!* I wanted to shout at my mother. *Do you believe me now?*

But, still, Mom wasn't ready to believe. She told Sara that Wayne had said my being on the dance team could have broken my hymen. Mom prodded that maybe all that activity could have caused the physical changes Sara was seeing. (Wayne had said that as a word of caution in my favor: the fact that I said I didn't bleed from Mitch penetrating me didn't mean that I was lying, and it didn't mean I had lost my virginity to someone else, either of which Mom seemed so desperate to prove.)

Sara made sure to clarify that dancing would not cause the amount of damage she saw. Nor would cheerleading or riding a bike or other exercise. Nor would tampons, even super-sized ones. This would all come up again later in court, many times. The tightness of my hymenal ring would be hotly debated.

I liked Sara's demeanor; she was very firm with my mother in a way I felt few others were willing to attempt. I would even call her aggressive—not in a mean way, but in the sense that she wasn't going to put up with Mom's nonsense. It was comforting for me to hear and, again, invigorating. She saw the truth. She knew. She believed me.

Mom didn't seem to know what to do with herself. She hardly said a word in response to Sara's findings. Her anger and stubborn ignorance didn't quite fit in this setting, faced with the blunt opinion of a medical professional.

As we left the appointment, Mom said to me, "You do realize this changes my life forever." There was more of her typical guilt-tripping in those words, more of her unique ability to make the situation all about her—but also, I thought, a glimmer of something else. I thought it meant she would believe me. I thought she meant her life was changing because Mitch was guilty.

Instead, it came to seem that that day was when she finalized her decision that she wasn't going to believe me. She continued with her same version of the story even after all that Sara had said. When, inevitably, people would later ask if I'd seen a gynecologist, Mom would tell them—including my own grandparents and uncle, asking out of genuine concern for me—that the exam had shown "basically nothing."

Again and again and again, somehow—stubbornly—Mom remained unconvinced. In fact, other than being annoyed with me and throwing herself more and more feverishly into her faith, she seemed altogether unfazed, unrattled by the bomb of the abuse shattering everything around us. She chose not to see it, to carry on with her life as if it could remain the same.

But that life didn't fit with the things I was saying. So, she stepped out of my life. It was as if she disappeared into a black hole. I think I suspected even then that she wouldn't be coming back.

About a month into the investigation, Aaron saw Mom at a football game that I was cheering for and told me that she met his eyes with a look that said, *I hate you.* She knew that he'd been interviewed by the detectives, just like she and Mitch and I all had been, and that his account supported mine. To the mother of a victim, that should have made him a friend—a hero, even. She should have been supporting him, sympathizing with him, thanking him. But it only made him an inconvenience to her. She associated him with all the stress and turmoil our family was immersed in, as if *he* were the one who had caused it, rather than the man she married.

She never talked to Aaron about this huge subject that now existed between us. Never once asked him about what I'd told him, what he'd seen or suspected. Never asked him if it was true. No one did except his mother and the investigators.

Mom was sitting in the bleachers with two girls, twin sisters, who were my best friends at the time, and their dad. When Aaron and his friends were making their way out of the stadium, the twins' dad followed them, stopping closely behind them each time they meandered, lingering while they chatted with other friends they'd run into. Aaron turned to check over his shoulder, trying to look casual, only to confirm that the man was staring at him. It was like he was a criminal being tracked. We think my mom asked him to follow Aaron, to watch him and make sure he wouldn't get the chance to talk to me. Since she knew Aaron would likely be called to testify in court as a witness, Mom didn't like me talking with him.

My boyfriend. My confidant. The whistleblower on crimes committed against me. Being kept away from me by my own mother.

At the time, I was frustrated by her power over me, wishing I could break free of it, and of course it stung to have such limited contact with Aaron, especially at such an emotional, disorienting time. With Mom keeping my cell phone away from me, Aaron and I went weeks, in the immediate aftermath of the report, without being able to talk much, if at all. I would borrow friends' phones to text him in whatever snippets I could. I needed his reassurance, his unparalleled willingness to listen.

Despite all of that, though, I didn't realize until much

later—until the battle ahead had toughened and enlightened me—that, by keeping us apart, Mom was grooming the situation in her own ways, just like Mitch had done for years. She was trying to remove what she saw as a barrier in her fight for Mitch's acquittal, to fabricate a situation that would give Mitch the best chances possible.

Again, this was only about a month after she'd first talked to Tommy and Wayne and claimed that she didn't know whom to believe.

It was around that same time that Mom hired herself a lawyer. It complicated everything moving forward. Nothing regarding the charges could develop without him being there; Tommy had to go through him instead of contacting Mom directly. Later on, after one of my testimonies in court, Nana asked Mom how she felt, and she replied that she couldn't answer that on the advice of her attorney. It was all so robotic, like she was no longer even human. She claimed she'd hired the lawyer to protect her rights as a mother, to ensure that she wouldn't lose Caleb or me. I could see the truth, though: she needed help in crafting how she was to be perceived, who she was supposed to be, an actor being coached in preparation for a role.

Similarly, Mom's insistence on labeling me as a liar, branding me with that invented sin, seemed to me to be her way of trying to control people's perceptions and mold a new version of the truth, one that placed me firmly in the role of *wrong* instead of *wronged*. If there was going to be a spotlight on me, she wanted to make sure it was the harshest light possible.

She was proactive about it. Methodical. My friends' parents would see the news about Mitch on TV and call her to ask about it; she formulated her responses in ways carefully calculated to drive a wedge between my friends and me, always portraying me as the untrustworthy one. Any time I had positive contact with anyone, she would contact them and try to turn them against me. I once saw Mitch's sister and her son in a store. She covered his eyes and said, "Don't look," like I was evil, a pariah.

I was surprised, at first, at how often Mom would talk to others about what had happened—the charges against Mitch, the ongoing trial, the fault lines dividing our family—but it was always her version of the story, presenting all of it as lies I had told, damage I had caused. She spent many hours on the phone, locked in her room, yet never talked to *me* about it or asked how I was doing. It was a confusing sort of torment to overhear those conversations, because a nagging voice in my head *did* think of this as damage I had caused, or had at least deepened. Before, I was the only one getting hurt. Now, my pain was a new kind, shaken vigorously with guilt and shame, and my family and all that was once familiar was crumbling down around me.

A few days before the first court date, my mom said to me, "You know you are the only one who can stop this."

I did know that—or, I should say, I did believe that to be true. Mitch also could have stopped the insanity by confessing to what he knew he had done. But at the time, I didn't see that as a real possibility. I could only see my continued pain and the pain that all of this was bringing to so many other people I cared about. Mom knew that was a point of weakness for me and used it as a weapon.

A friend sent me a care package, and Mom thrust it at me, saying, "Not that you really need it." That doubt creeped in again—*was* I undeserving? Had I caused more harm than good? Just after Mitch was arrested, we watched videos in school as part of a campaign against drunk driving that emphasized how awful prison was. Thinking about Mitch being there—even though part of me knew he deserved to be —weighed on me a lot. Caleb missed his dad so much, and he and Mom didn't hesitate to make me feel like that was all my doing.

It's crushing to acknowledge how much my mother thickened the self-deprecation that Mitch had already built up in me in impermeable layers. Abuse leaves its victims feeling dirty, ashamed, inadequate. Instead of consoling me and helping me to rebuild from those voids, my mother created new ones all her own.

A Rescue

THAT FEBRUARY, FOUR MONTHS AFTER MITCH'S ARREST, Nana and Poppy finally found out the truth—the terrible truth that they had long suspected but had desperately wanted to be wrong about. Mom had managed to dodge their questions and limit their contact with me for all that time, but I don't know how she expected to keep them in the dark forever. From the beginning, seeing how little support either of us was going to get from my mother, Tommy had asked her if there were other family members he could reach out to, maybe the grandparents in New York whom he'd heard mention of. He presented it like a favor; he would take on some of the burden of these difficult conversations, be the bearer of the bad news, bridge the communication gap that had widened across years and miles and secrets. But Mom dismissed it immediately, saying that I wouldn't want him to tell my grandparents what was going on.

Thankfully, Tommy isn't the type to sit quietly when he knows things aren't right. Those past few months, we'd spent a lot of time together at the police station and the courthouse.

Being in court involves a lot of waiting around; there are always so many cases going on at once and so many people in and out, and my attorney was sometimes tied up with matters that I didn't need to be, or couldn't be, a part of. Tommy always had other matters to tend to as well, but he let me tag along. I had nowhere else to go. It was often only Tommy at my side—doing his best to counsel and comfort me, the only person there to testify on my behalf and corroborate my story —all while my mother stood beside my rapist and his team. While my anger about that churned deep inside me, buried under many layers, Tommy's burned much closer to the surface. I could see his frustration growing throughout those long winter months.

"We need someone on your team!" he sighed. There was a bit of a pleading tone to it, a weariness. He carried so much of the burden—willingly, it always seemed. He had such a deeply rooted sense of responsibility and loyalty to victims like me. He'd become like my guardian. But of course it took a toll, and all the more so because of the toll he could see it was taking on me.

After stewing about it in his office late one night, he started digging around online, hoping to connect the right dots to my relatives in New York. Because I was a minor, he had to run a lot of things past my mom, who wasn't looking to divulge information, and, still so heavily under her influence, I wasn't much help either. So he had next to nothing to guide him—no names, no contact information. Plus, as I'd learned through repeated experience, there's a common misconception in the South that "New York" automatically means Manhattan. A sleepy little town like Westbridge wouldn't be a blip on anyone's radar. His impassioned hunt worked, though; he found my uncle, one of Mom's brothers, and called him.

In that instant, everything changed.

My uncle called Nana and Poppy. It was late; they were both in bed. He gave Poppy some vague story about needing help with work he was doing on his truck, to get him to come over. Sometimes these kinds of words need to be spoken face to face. Once Poppy knew the scope of what they were dealing with—that the problem was not a faulty truck engine but something much, much bigger—he went home to get Nana and bring her back there with him. Nana, of course, immediately panicked, her thoughts rushing to all sorts of disastrous possibilities. And she wasn't wrong. No one had died, exactly, but the family was forever changed. The Jessica she knew and the Mitch she wanted to know were now shaped by these permanent markings, victim and abuser, confirming that the shadows she'd long thought she saw drawn over us were real. This is how the image of me changes for so many people once they know my story. I'm so fortunate that it didn't change a thing about how Nana and Poppy treated me, other than to amplify the qualities I already cherished so much about them—their warm aura of nurturing, of safety.

Tommy calls their involvement a life-changer, and that's no exaggeration. Much like the chain of phone calls set in motion once Aaron knew the truth, these widening ripples were a bit unsettling at first but quickly delivered exactly what I'd been needing.

Right away, Nana texted Mom, asking her to call if she was still awake. And just like that, the roadblocks Mom had constructed between two realms of my life were knocked down. Now my grandparents knew. Now they were talking about it. It was no longer this thing hidden in a corner closet that Mom hoped no one would ever open.

But, of course, that didn't mean she could admit the truth.

She told Nana that I was lying about Mitch, that I'd been going wild and hanging out with older college boys. She told my uncle the same things when he told her he'd heard from Tommy. Thankfully, they knew me well enough to know that that behavior didn't sound like me.

Nana told Mom she needed to talk to me directly in the morning and that she would know if I was lying. Fiercely protective, Nana had always had a strong intuition about these things. She could connect with children, especially me, on an honest, instinctive level; she didn't talk down to kids but leveled with us, human to human. Which, I'm sure, was precisely why my mom had done everything she could to keep us out of contact.

At that moment, though, I think Mom knew that she didn't have a choice. Things were shifting enough, with so many more people involved, that her footing wasn't quite so solid. Enough elements of the game had changed that she didn't seem as sure of her next move. Still, as she told me that next morning that Nana wanted to talk to me, she thrust her phone at me with an angry sort of reluctance. A resignation.

I hesitated, not yet knowing all that had unfolded overnight while I slept—wondering if this call would really be any different, wondering how much I could get away with saying.

But before I had said much of anything, I heard in my ear —slowly, deliberately, emphatically, because she knew how important it was that I truly *hear* it—"Nana believes you."

Referring to herself in the third person like that, a habit of Nana's, was particularly reassuring in that moment. The simple sound of those repeating syllables, *Nana*, was innately comforting, and it emphasized her role as the maternal protector I needed. It was such a stark contrast to the responses coming at me from every other direction.

In that instant, a wall inside me broke open, and I cried in a way Nana says she'd never heard before. It was such an immense relief that she finally knew the truth, and that she'd offered her support to me immediately, that I could feel myself breathing deeper as I sucked in air between sobs. Now I had an ally on the inside. Nana knew me better than anyone; she could corroborate my story, fill in gaps where my memory was hazy, help Tommy and my attorney and me build a stronger case. Just as she'd done already with that phone call, I knew she would be there throughout the fight ahead to hold me up when I had trouble staying strong and believing. I no longer felt so hopelessly alone in all of this.

I gave the phone back to my mom, wondering if things would be different between us now. Would she see the importance of this lifeline I had just grabbed on to? Now that someone else believed me, could she manage to as well?

Nana told her right away that I was telling the truth. In that moment, Mom seemed to understand, or at least seemed willing to consider that the truth could be very different from what she'd been proclaiming. Maybe that shift I'd been feeling that morning was real and would last. I kept holding onto that hope.

A few days later, Nana and Poppy made the drive from New York to Tennessee, the first of many such trips they would make over the long months of uncertainty that stretched before us. Twelve hours each way.

Their arrival felt like a rescue. They stayed at a hotel nearby, and I eagerly took that opportunity to escape and stayed with them throughout their visit. The past several months had thrown all of my usual torment into overdrive, and I could hardly get my bearings. Nana told me they knew right away that "of course" they needed to get to me; this is what's supposed to be done for family. She and Poppy were devastated by learning of the charges against Mitch because of what it all meant for *me*, not for him. Yet, it was not as shocking of a development for them as it seemed to be for so many others, since they'd been uncomfortable about his presence in my life from so early on. And now that the truth was out in the open, they knew that Mom and Mitch and their cohort were isolating me and doing everything they could to break me down in the hope that I would retract my statement. It always helped to hear others vocalize things like that, things that I was gaslighted into believing were just me being crazy. Being with my grandparents provided some much-needed shelter from the storm that my daily life had become.

Still, I could never fully relax. I was skittish, like a frightened animal. Every night, I would ask Poppy to make sure the door was locked. Eventually, he put a table in front of the door to give me an added layer of safety.

The only way I could fall asleep was to have Nana hold me, wrapping her arms around my upper body as if she were cradling a baby. With one ear nestled into the soft reassurance of her body, I needed her to cover my other ear with her hand, to block the anticipation of Mitch's nauseating whispers. No matter how deeply I had tried to burrow into the bed, pulling the sheets up over the side of my face as I curled up tight, I couldn't shut that feeling out. I would often wake myself up from violent jerking and kicking, the kind of startle some people might experience when they dream they're falling. That had become the norm for me. I don't remember what I was dreaming about, thankfully—if I even was dreaming at all—but the mere act of falling asleep left me feeling vulnerable and afraid. It was too hard for my body and my mind to relax and shake off all that had happened to me, and nighttime brought such quiet stillness that those demons would come rushing in to center focus.

It breaks my heart to think of the things that Nana had to experience during those long nights. It wasn't until I read the notes she'd written up for the office of the district attorney (DA), many months later, that I realized just how bad it was. She wrote that my sleep patterns were "very disturbing." That my body would jerk so hard that it would lift me right off the mattress, sometimes propelling me to sit up. That I would whimper or cry for hours, even after I'd dozed off. She was always there to reassure me that I was safe and coax me back to sleep, which means either that she was already awake, waiting on alert, or that I was continually waking her up too. I suspect she went that entire visit without a good night's sleep. And it must have been hard to remain calm and soothing when she was so angry at Mitch and my mother for all that they had done, and *not* done, to leave me in this state.

Early one morning, Nana and Poppy's faces were creased with worry as they asked me, gently, if I remembered what had happened during the night. I did remember the first part. My back had been hurting (one of several common pains I had in those days; Mitch would push against my back when assaulting me while I was lying on my stomach, which had left a lingering feeling like needles poking into my spine), and Nana had rubbed some Icy Hot ointment on it, the slow, soothing motion eventually lulling me to sleep. They said I'd then slept for three hours—a long stretch for me in those days. But what I didn't remember was that, throughout those three hours, I tossed around so violently that I sometimes jerked forward, sitting up, and looked frantically around the room. They said I looked terrified. Then I would lie down again and immediately be asleep. I was probably sleeping the entire time.

"You didn't even see us," Poppy said, his voice strained.

He looked like he had seen a ghost. My ghosts were now haunting others as well.

The tension was affecting Aaron too; like me, he was always on edge, wondering who he might run into, how much they knew, and how they'd treat him. Being associated with me at that time had the potential to make anyone be looked at differently, and poor Aaron more than most, since he was dating me *and* was the one who'd reported the abuse. He might as well have been carrying a banner that said, "I'm with Jessica!" If we were lucky, the looks we'd get from others—even some who were strangers to us but evidently knew who *we* were—could be pitying or on occasion genuinely concerned. But they more often felt suspicious or critical. Any one of those looks branded us as "other," as if we were marked somehow. I often felt out of place in my once familiar town, like I was just passing through from another realm.

Even when people didn't seem to be looking at me—and when a rational mind could have told me that they truly weren't—I always suspected that they secretly were. Maybe I'd pass by a mother walking her daughter out after cheer-leading practice, a girl in a different grade whom I didn't know well, and they'd be talking about errands they needed to run on the way home, as if the world were still rotating normally on its axis, as if the days were still passing at their usual speed. With my head cast down, I'd watch them discreetly as I passed by, my eyes fixated to the side until they hurt. They'd be looking at each other, not seeming to pay any attention to me or the others meandering around them. But I always had the feeling that they allowed themselves to look at me only after I'd passed by, whispering. The girl would lean close to her mom and say, "That's the girl I told you about." I'd be *that girl*, the one they'd all heard about. Now they'd have a face and a body to associate with the name and the story.

Of course, the other thing that set my skin prickling when I passed by parents and their teenage kids together, especially mothers and daughters, was jealousy. I wished I could lean in close to my mother and share secrets with her, plan out errands together, maybe stop for ice cream on the way home or plan a girls' day out on the weekend. If I were out somewhere with my mother, it only felt like there were even more eyes on me, and never the sympathetic ones. If Aaron's imaginary sign said, "I'm with Jessica!" my mother's said, "Don't believe her," with a big arrow pointing in my direction. It felt like she was one of the ones whispering, at any chance she got, and often not even trying to be subtle about it.

It was no wonder I left the house as little as possible.

Aaron called me as he left the grocery store one day, telling me about how he'd rounded a corner to see Mitch just down the aisle. It was like a moment from a scary movie, designed to make you jump. They made eye contact, but then Aaron walked away. I knew he felt helpless in all of this, too, wishing he could channel that anger into some sort of solution.

I think it was inevitable that, that summer, almost a year after that unassuming movie night changed both our lives, Aaron and I broke up, a natural and amicable parting after all that we'd endured. While we were still together, as he tried to navigate that helplessness, I kept reminding him of what a difference he'd already made by speaking up for me in the first place. If it weren't for him, I didn't know how much longer the abuse would have gone on. But I think he wished he could have known and stopped it sooner. This immense gift he'd given me would never be enough in his eyes.

I hated that Aaron had to be on edge like I did, while

trying to do something as simple as grocery shopping with his mom. And more than anything I hated that my rapist was free to wander the aisles of the supermarket, getting ingredients for dinner like he was just a normal guy, a caring dad getting ready to cook for his family. Did he feel everyone's eyes analyzing and criticizing him the way I did? Was his head filled with imaginary whispers? I hoped so.

After the incident at the hotel, Nana tried to talk to Mom about what a hard time I was having sleeping, describing how I would jerk around and startle awake. Mom said dismissively that I had always done that—which was, at best, complete ignorance and, at worst, yet another blatant lie. I was a child in distress, and she continued to turn away.

When Mom would stop by the hotel room to visit, she would resume her habit of searching through my stuff, right there in front of Nana and Poppy. She'd dump my entire purse out onto the bed and rifle through the money and makeup, looking for who knows what—anything that she thought could be used against me, I guess.

I savored small comforts while I was staying with my grandparents—small comforts that, to me, seemed huge. It was rejuvenating to know I would have three good meals each day while they were there to look after me. I couldn't remember the last time I'd had three meals in a day; sometimes I was lucky to piece together one. I often went to school without a lunch or money to buy one. If my friends asked why I wasn't eating, I would just tell them I wasn't hungry. Meanwhile, my stomach felt like it was collapsing in on itself. I hoped that if I said I wasn't hungry often enough, I could convince myself it was true.

And it was freeing just to be able to lounge around the hotel room in my pajamas without a bra on. Ever since I first started developing breasts—around the same time Mitch had started abusing me—Mom had insisted that I needed to wear a bra at all times, including to bed. I remember it felt like a little bit of a risk, then, when I asked Nana, after I'd been staying at the hotel for a couple nights, if I needed to sleep with a bra on.

Nana looked confused. "No," she said. "You should sleep comfortably."

Being with them eased the tension I'd been carrying throughout my body. It had become so constant that I wasn't even always aware of it, but now I was hyper aware of the change as it faded, like when you can feel a headache starting to ease up.

Nana and Poppy had been planning to head home to New York after a few days. The night before they were going to leave, they suggested taking me home so they could head out early the next morning. As I heard the words coming out of Nana's mouth, it was like her voice started getting farther and farther away, like I was sinking slowly down into a deep hole. In staying with them, I had so eagerly enclosed myself in a bubble that I wanted to at least pretend was impenetrable; I was happy to avoid the reality that raged outside those walls and hope that it would somehow change while I was away. Being with them made me feel like all of this chaos wasn't really happening, or at least like I had some allies in it. I wasn't so alone and afraid, having them in my corner. And now they were leaving.

Instinctively, my body curled up on itself, retracting into the smallest shape possible. I wanted to crawl inside myself, into a shell no one else could get into. My senses shut down; I could no longer hear or see Nana, couldn't see the sunlight streaming into the room or feel the starchy bedspread I was lying on. Everything was fading quickly away, and I wanted it to keep fading and not come back. *Don't make me go back to her*, I wanted to say. *Don't make me face all of this.* But I didn't say anything. I couldn't speak. I didn't want to have to think or feel anymore.

This was a lot like the panicking dread I used to feel when leaving from my visits in New York—but even worse, because now we had entered this disorienting new world where the demons were out in public and couldn't be ignored.

Seeing that they couldn't leave me in that state to face those demons, Nana and Poppy stayed another two weeks.

One day during their visit, Mom mentioned that she needed laundry detergent. I think she was just thinking out loud, reminding herself to put it on her grocery list, but Nana and Poppy, ever the helpers, said they'd take us to the store to browse around and stock up and offered to cover the cost themselves. Mom packed a cart with two hundred dollars' worth of stuff—nice things like steaks that she wouldn't often spring for—and then took it all with her to Mitch's dad's apartment. Poor Nana and Poppy had been hoping they were doing *me* a favor, ensuring that the kitchen would be well supplied and that I would continue to eat better after they had to go home. I wasn't at all surprised by Mom's behavior so tried to just shrug it off. I told my grandparents I could go days without eating much. "I've done it before," I said.

A few days later, I had to stop by the apartment to meet with a social worker who had been helping with my case. I had been staying at the hotel for a week at that point, and coming home felt peculiar, like walking through a museum exhibit where people's belongings have been preserved just like they'd left them years ago. I felt a few degrees removed from it all, like none of it was really mine anymore.

The social worker first wanted to talk to Mom alone, and, as I waited, I found myself drawn into my parents' bedroom, sort of like a boomerang coming back to where it was thrown from, but in slow motion. I lay down on the bed and curled up on my side, wanting to shrink away completely. I could smell Mitch's shampoo on the sheets, sandalwood and something slightly floral—a scent that, still today, instantly ushers me back to that apartment, that slice of time, and wraps me in a feeling of home; not just a scent but an experience, a sensation that swells up to fill my entire core. I'm sure he had been there while I was gone, probably leaving just shortly before I got there that night. He wasn't allowed to be around me while the investigation was going on, but I knew he visited often while I was away. Months later, a court order would specify that, in preparation for my return from a visit with Nana and Poppy in New York, my mother "must assure that all sights and scents" of my stepfather's presence were "eliminated from the family home."

Breathing in his scent was the strangest mix of pain and comfort. How could someone who had brought so much damage into my life be the person I most wished I could talk to in that moment? It was a different version of him I was longing for, the one I had thought was my friend. A long-gone version. I wished the thought of him didn't make me so sad and angry. I wished I could transport us all back to a simpler time, when none of this was happening—although, if I were being honest with myself, when would that even have been? I didn't know a time before Mitch and could hardly remember one before the abuse. I had to push that thought away; I needed at least the imaginary escape to better days. I wanted to sink down, down, down into a deep, dreamless sleep there on that bed and wake up days later to find myself in a different life.

Nana and Poppy could see how unhealthy it was for me to remain in Tennessee, especially to think of my living back in the apartment, largely alone, once they'd have to go back home. I was always surrounded by reminders of what Mitch had done to me and what my mom continued *not* to do for me. I was fending for myself, living in the scene of the crime.

"Maybe you should come back to New York," Nana said to my mom, just gently enough that it sounded like a warm invitation but just firmly enough that it sounded like one that shouldn't be turned down. "We'll help you get set up with a place to live, help with the kids, whatever you need. You could be back where your family is."

Mom said she would think about it, but I think we all knew that her words were empty gestures. It was all just a part of her charade, pretending not to know whom to believe.

Many of my memories of those days are disjointed pieces, and I'm not sure where some of them fit. But I know at some point Nana emphasized to Mom that, were we to move to New York, my bedroom furniture could not come with us. I knew that by saying that, she was saying, *You can't bring those memories. You can't continue to surround her with that trauma.* And therefore also saying, *Jessica is telling the truth. You need to believe her and help her.*

I don't know if I could have made it through those dark days without Nana and Poppy. When they did eventually have to head back to New York, the broken pieces of me felt much closer to the surface, but already I felt stronger from having spent so much time in their company. Now that the full truth was out, and they'd seen my new reality firsthand, our bond was stronger than ever, and I knew they'd continue to fight with me and for me, even from a distance.

Nana insisted on the importance of us keeping in contact and bought me a cell phone, seeing how unlikely it was that I would ever get mine back from Mom. She was furious that I hadn't had one in case of emergencies, at the very least, especially now that she knew how often I was left by myself. She and Poppy were the people I called most often—which I'm sure was precisely one of the reasons Mom didn't want me to have one. Our conversations were a remedy I turned to when I was having a down day, feeling hungry or alone.

Nana would try to talk me through what to look for so I could cook, but the cupboards were pathetically empty, and we often couldn't come up with much, if anything, to put together. There might be a little peanut butter but no bread, a little orange juice in the fridge. Nana said we were going to have to be sneaky in order to get me some nutrition.

She started sending me care packages with food and hidden money, some flashes of green revealing themselves as I flipped through cocoa packets. Sometimes she would order pizza to be delivered to me, which was a welcome treat, but a scandalous one—I'd always be careful to take the packaging and any leftovers out to the dumpster, in order to avoid one of Mom's outbursts. She had put on a dramatic show of anger when Nana sent me an Edible Arrangement, because she hadn't sent anything for Caleb. I told them I would share it with them, but Mom wanted nothing to do with it since it had come from Nana, like it was tainted or something. Nana also sent me a new laptop for school, which I desperately needed, and Mom sent it back.

Mom loved a good spectacle and was well versed in creating them. Once, I was on the phone with Nana, and Mom ripped the phone away from me and started yelling (whether at Nana or at me—but loud enough so that she knew Nana would hear through the wildly gesticulated phone—who knows. She was always so loud). A neighbor called the police. Mom called her lawyer, Mitch's lawyer,

Tommy, and a bunch of her friends to come over at the same time. She was putting on a show. She could never just have an argument with one person; she was always getting as many people involved as possible. Embarrassment was good discipline in her eyes. She told the cops that I had choked her and lifted her up against the wall. What am I, the Hulk? I can't even lift my dog! Mom was doing all she could think of to portray me as uncontrollable.

Amidst the chaos, Mom did occasionally show affection toward me, but in such limited and seemingly random ways that it felt like a cat-and-mouse game, and I could never fully trust it, as much as I may have wanted to. About a week into Nana and Poppy's visit, after we'd had plenty of cold receptions and awkward interactions from Mom, she had started texting me to say that she loved me, calling me precious, saying goodnight and tacking on a little "Love, Mom" signature. It was welcome and uncomfortable and hard to process, all at the same time. I couldn't remember the last time I'd heard my mom say she loved me. I wished it would last. I wished it were enough.

Devil Be Gone

NECESSITY KEPT MOM AND ME INVOLVED IN EACH other's lives to some extent, at least for the first couple years after the truth came out. I was fifteen when the abuse was reported, so I didn't have a driver's license. It was Mom who drove me to the DA's office for my first meeting with Laural, the attorney assigned to my case. Neither of us had met her before. Mom dropped me off and left me there alone.

The DA's office, which in hindsight I understand to be terribly underfunded, was in a basement, with papers strewn everywhere. It was a visual representation of the disarray in my brain. I was afraid to ask any questions—I wouldn't even have known what to ask. I needed someone there beside me.

I didn't understand why I was there that day. I didn't know Laural was a lawyer. I thought she was another police officer of some sort. There were so many people I met in such a short amount of time, and nobody really told me what they were there for or what they were supposed to be doing for me. If they tried to, it must have just disintegrated in the fog that filled my mind. I was functioning on autopilot, at best:

entering rooms, sitting in chairs, speaking when spoken to. Laural was just another person interviewing me, another suit I was supposed to open up to, making me repeat so much of the same information I'd already given to Aaron, Tommy, Colleen, Lisa, and Sara. I didn't even realize at first that Laural was someone who was going to try to help me! Mom had left me there blindly, and I had followed mutely. It had become our routine.

Likewise, the first time Laural walked me into a courtroom, for the preliminary hearing, I didn't have a grasp on what was happening, didn't even realize we would be heading into a formal court session, in front of a judge, for hours of proceedings. The lingo was like a foreign language to me, and, at that point, things were spilling forward quickly. That first hearing was just a few weeks after the abuse had been reported. I was still just going through the motions, following and nodding, trying not to feel like I was drowning. I was using the coping mechanism I'd learned during the abuse, simply focusing on getting through each day, one little snippet at a time. Comprehending the bigger picture was impossible. I kept my head down and kept quiet as much as possible. I was always listening or replying, never asking. I know now that I should have been doing a lot more asking.

I should have asked, for instance, why Mom left me alone again at Laural's office the morning of that hearing. She went to meet up with Mitch and their friends at the courthouse and had me walk there with Laural. We had met only the one time before that. I'm sure Laural tried to be reassuring—and I'm sure she felt sorry for me—but we were essentially strangers, and the few minutes it took to walk to court were awkward, peppered with silences. The clicking of her high heels on the sidewalk thrummed in my jumbled mind.

I understand the logistics of the judicial process a bit

more now, after seeing the sum of the parts, but thankfully it feels largely like having crammed for an exam that I'll never have to take again. The preliminary hearing determines whether there's enough of a case to move forward. If there is, the evidence is then presented to a grand jury, who decides whether to indict. By the time Tommy presented our case to the grand jury, his investigation had brought about many more charges, on which Mitch was indicted and therefore was arrested again and had to make bond again. The charges stemming from the indictment are then argued for and against in the trial. Because I was a minor, and because the Department of Children's Services (DCS) had issued a no-contact order between Mitch and me, there was also a juvenile court hearing in between the preliminary hearing and the trial, to determine whether it was in my best interests to stay at home or somewhere else. That part was out of Laural's hands and was instead handled by DCS, so I had more new names and faces to learn there. DCS wanted to make sure to keep either me or Mitch out of the apartment, to ensure my safety.

Tommy and Wayne were at the juvenile court hearing and were questioned after I was; in addition to a couple of attorneys working on my behalf, we were questioned by Mitch's attorney and my mother's attorney. As I was grilled for hours, it was hard to tell that that hearing was supposed to be designed to protect me. It was a preview of what the trial would be like, years later, as the defense team gathered up all they could to use against me. Laural wasn't allowed to be there and so was only brought up to speed after the fact, and she was livid; she said Mitch's and Mom's lawyers had gone way above and beyond what they needed to ask, scheming to embarrass me and trip me up by asking about every single incident of abuse. Nana and Poppy weren't allowed to be in there with me either. It often felt like Tommy, Wayne, and I were the outcasts in the room, rather than a victim and her protectors.

Meanwhile, Laural was working to build our case. After the preliminary hearing, there are a lot of other types of hearings that take place before the trial, smaller matters leading into the big one that she and the defense team would have to hash out. One was about the "It is what it is" answer that Mitch had given when Tommy and Wayne first questioned him at the police station. The judge wouldn't allow it to be discussed in the trial, and in fact dismissed that entire recorded interview, because it was too ambiguous and might be too prejudicial—after all, a defendant is presumed innocent until proven guilty. I know I'm not a lawyer, but a statement like that certainly seems like proof of guilt to me. Laural said she didn't understand how an admission of guilt was excluded, either. There was also a lot of debate leading up to the trial about the extent to which I could talk about my living situation and family dynamics, such as how my mom was treating me. The defense didn't want it brought up. Laural had to push that it would be pretty difficult to get through the case without talking about my family dynamics.

This is how four years passed before the trial. It could take months to get through each little motion or suppression or appeal. From my perspective at the time, the terminology and logistics of the many-stepped process didn't matter; they were all just different pieces of a terrible thing. I had to be on the stand for too many hours, had to listen and watch and wait as too many others lied and discussed too many deeply personal details about my life.

Thankfully, I learned early on in the process what an advocate Laural would be for me as we headed into battle together. I had been so timid even in speaking to her, one on one; how could I face a courtroom of strangers and ex-supporters and find words for these awful things? As I followed her into the courthouse the morning of the preliminary hearing, feeling like a tourist or a lost child, I willed myself to trust that her powerful voice could speak for me and help me find my own, to haul it out from underneath all the commotion, stress, and fear.

We were both immediately put to the test and confronted with the raw truth of what we'd be up against, as we came across my mom and her church friends in the courthouse hallway, talking and laughing and ignoring me completely. I was there to testify that my mother's husband had been raping and sexually abusing me for years, and she acted as if my presence there had nothing to do with her, or as if I weren't there at all.

Then, while I was testifying, laying out the details of how her husband had touched me and violated me, my mom was sitting in the back of the courtroom, playing with her nails, whispering loudly to her friends, and laughing. She was *laughing*. This went on for several hours.

After the hearing was over, I found myself waiting awkwardly in the hallway again while Mom had her social hour, like we'd just been through a bizarre time warp that looped us right back to where we'd started. Laural click-clacked in her heels over to Mom and said, "You know this is your daughter, right? Are you gonna take her home?"

Any question or façade there had been before as to whose side my mother was on had crumbled that day, and, in its wake, I knew then that Laural, like Tommy, would be the kind of ally I needed. They saw how alone I was and witnessed firsthand the opposition my family was mounting against me. Laural has described Mom's behavior as worse than just a lack of support—as total *anti*-support. She did not participate at all in Laural's quest to figure out what had happened to me or how to help me.

There would be many other court dates in the years ahead that ended with me standing out in tall-ceilinged, echoing courthouse hallways with just Laural or Tommy by my side. Once, I told Laural I wanted to wait out there for Mom to come talk to me. I was so sure she would. I waited and waited. And then I went home.

———

Mom's gossipy laughter in the courtroom proved to be the beginning of a trend. She and her friends would gang up and taunt me like high school bullies—a confusing and seemingly counterintuitive move, as I'm pretty sure she met most of them in Bible study and prayer groups. She'd started collecting new friends quite suddenly after Mitch's arrest, women I'd never heard of before. They just started appearing. She seemed to rally them around her like troops.

Once, after I flew home from a visit to New York, Mom picked me up at the Nashville airport with her friend Barb in tow—a strategic move, as if she needed reinforcements—and the two of them talked about Mom and Mitch's wedding throughout the forty-minute drive home: what a beautiful day it had been, how much fun everyone had had, what a fairytale romance theirs was, blessed by God.

I was jetting off to Nana and Poppy's house as much as I could in those days. It felt like a necessity, like medication; it was the only way I could latch onto some bit of sanity. Staying with them gave me the type of comfort I had been needing so desperately, free of judgment or ulterior motives. I knew they truly wanted what was best for me, believed me, and would do whatever they could to help and protect me. It was such a refreshing change of pace from my day-to-day life in Tennessee that I could hardly trust that it was real—and it made me even more viscerally aware of all that was lacking at home.

Mom brought Barb along again for another airport pickup a few months later. In the car that day, Barb said she had seen a story on the news about a girl who wore a bikini under her clothes at the airport and stripped down when going through security, walking through the scanners in just her skimpy bathing suit. Over her shoulder, hurled at me in the back seat, Barb said, "That sounds like something you would do."

Mom said nothing. She just let me sit there, with that comment hanging in the air, as my face burned. In what was a common cycle in those days, I first felt the sharp sting of anger, then the slower, deeper blaze of shame, even though my rational mind knew the dirty feeling that was always with me was not due to any actions of my own. I was not the promiscuous troublemaker they kept trying to portray me as, but they often succeeded in making me feel like one. I heard my own voice among the echoes of their taunts in my head.

When we got home, Mom went to bed without asking me how my trip was or even asking if I was hungry. I poured myself some cereal and sat alone in the kitchen, my slow crunching the only sound in the house.

Barb's comment reminded me of a time Mom and I were at the mall and I saw some cute bra-and-underwear sets on a mannequin in the rue21 window. I was desperately in need of new underwear, just like with the rest of my clothes. But Mom made a *tsk* sound and glared at me, appalled.

"Why do you need that kind if no one is seeing them?" she shot at me.

They were fun, colorful patterns, aimed precisely at

teenage girls like me. They were the kinds of things my friends were all wearing. It's not like I was asking for lacy push-up bras from Victoria's Secret. But once again, I was left feeling ashamed for having asked.

Sometimes Mom would pull Caleb in on her catty acts, too. He was twelve years old as the investigation started, and he adored his father; he was easily influenced into accepting Mom and Mitch's version of the world. Just as I had been when the abuse started, he was young and naïve enough that he wouldn't even have known what questions to ask or had any basis of understanding for the horrible things being talked about. He just knew his dad was in trouble and that it was my fault. I never stood a chance in overcoming his perception of me as the evil one.

Caleb was in the living room with Mom and me one day when, trying to power through the tension and carry on with my existence, I told Mom about a boy I had a crush on at school. Immediately, I wished I hadn't said anything.

Mom turned to Caleb and said, "You are a witness that she just said she likes a boy."

A witness. As if documenting what I was saying—why? Because she thought I'd change my story later? Like I was setting up some sort of trick? She was lining up defenses, including my own brother, making sure he stayed on her side of the line she'd drawn between us. It was always there, as if physically dividing the room the way teenagers do when they have to share a bedroom and are fighting over the territory. Sometimes the line was so tangible I felt like it was physically repelling me away from her, that if I got too close, I would trip over it. With the matter of a few words, Mom could so easily put me right back where she wanted me, in the corner, with fingers pointing at me accusingly, all while solidifying Caleb's perception that I was fundamentally untrustworthy.

One Monday that November was a marathon of a bad day, with one incident after another of intimidation and shaming from my alleged support network. If Tommy could have had a camera on us, he would have been screaming at it as the evidence poured in against my mom's claims that I was being well cared for.

As Mom drove me to the courthouse that morning, Grandpa John rode along in the car with us. It was his birthday that day, and he loudly griped that it was going to be the worst birthday of his life. This was an accusation against me for spoiling things, not a lament about the things his son had done.

When Mom picked me up from court that afternoon to take me to school, the illustrious Barb was along for the ride. I guess neither one of them wanted to miss the chance for drama. Since I didn't want to wear my dressy courtroom clothes to school, I had brought some jeans and a T-shirt with me in a bag. I asked Mom if I could change in the car. I had a tank top on under my sweater, so changing my shirt wasn't going to expose anything, and I could have discreetly changed my pants while sitting down. No one passing by was going to see anything.

Barb sounded horrified. "No—I don't want to be accused of anything!" she squawked.

Once again, Mom didn't say anything to defend me. I should have been used to it by then, but in some ways the shock only compounded into disbelief as time went on, as her offenses added up.

It was well past lunch by the time we left the courthouse. I'd be heading right into a few hours of classes and then dance team practice, but Mom didn't offer me anything to eat. I hadn't eaten all day. This was another norm that only got worse with time.

I got home from dance around 5:30, tired and ravenous. I walked into my bedroom, eager to change and then go scrounge up some food, only to find my entire room torn apart. Mom had pulled the clothes out from all of my dresser drawers—everything, down to socks, bras, and underwear—and left it all littered across my floor. The pockets of every pair of pants were turned inside out. I don't even know what she was looking for, and there would be no rational explanation if I asked her.

This had simply become my reality: always accused, always on edge, and always pretty sure it would just keep getting worse.

After each of my meetings with Laural, Mom would question me about what we'd talked about. It felt not only invasive but belittling, as if there really shouldn't have been anything we would need to address. She kept waiting and watching eagerly for me to crack under the pressure.

Despite the many attempts by my mother and her cohort to get me to change my story, I never seriously considered that an option. I knew I was telling the truth, no matter how much they didn't want to believe it. In fact, the more they refuted me, the more I knew I had to continue my fight. Of course, that fight was exhausting, so it was tempting at times to just give up. Mitch had already smothered my confidence for years, and now my own mother and brother and so many others were only adding to that burden instead of helping me through it. But, most of the time, I could call upon the anger I felt about that as a source of strength, rather than letting it all drag me down. Plus, it pains me to admit, I kept thinking my mom would eventually understand and come around to my side—especially since I was pretty sure she had long known the truth herself. I just kept waiting for her to be willing to admit it.

I had also started meeting with a counselor, but Mom had to make that a source of conflict, too. She knew Wednesdays were the best days for my appointments, as that was the one weekday when I didn't have dance practice. But she continually scheduled my appointments on other days, which meant I had to leave practice early and then wasn't allowed to perform with the team at Friday night football games. It was yet another punishment, keeping me away from my social outlet, from something that made me happy.

The counseling was court mandated, and for a long time it felt more like a chore than a helpful outlet. Beyond the scheduling issues, I struggled to find a good rapport with anyone, and I bounced from one counselor to the next every few months. One left after finishing her internship, and it felt like any progress we had started to make was a waste, just to have to start all over again with somebody new. Another knew my mom well, so she was far from impartial. I continued to go to the appointments; given the court mandate, I didn't really have a choice, and I also wanted to show that I was taking all of this seriously and making an effort toward healing. But I never felt like I was making much progress, just going through the motions and waiting for them to make some sort of difference.

While Nana had been in town, she'd gone with me to one of my counseling appointments and told the therapist about the lack of care—food, medicine, compassion—I was getting from my mom. It wasn't something I'd spoken up about, at least not much. Like so many other elements of my life at that time, I glossed over it, not wanting to stir up any more tension at home, wanting to just wish it all away. The day after that session with Nana, Mom got a call from Child Protective Services (CPS), whom my counselor had contacted out of concern for my welfare. They had Mom go in for a meeting with some of their social workers to try to get a better sense of our situation at home. Nana and Poppy both went, too—and, as if to even out the sides, Mom brought along several of her church friends.

One of those friends, Ruth, said aloud during the meeting one of the ugly truths that had been palpable, just barely below the surface, for those many long, lonely months: that she'd told my mother from the beginning that her responsibility was to her husband.

It was what propelled them all forward, blindly insisting that Mitch was innocent. In their eyes, he had to be. They were unwilling to consider any possibility outside of that. I see it all as a continuation of the charade Mom had started crafting when I was just a kid and Mitch adopted me. Marrying Mitch and having Caleb had been important building blocks for her fairytale family. Mitch adopting me made a prettier picture out of her teenage pregnancy and rocky start at motherhood. She'd given herself a fresh start in a new state. And now she wanted so badly to maintain that perfect family image that she was willing to fake it, at any cost.

When Ruth said that, Nana noticed a CPS worker's eyebrows rise as she started writing notes. The woman later told Nana that she'd been thinking, *Shouldn't the children come first?* But that shift had started in my mother shortly after we'd moved to Tennessee. Typically such an outspoken woman, unwilling to tolerate nonsense from anyone, she had gradually become subservient to what Mitch wanted. Mom and Nana may have disagreed on many things over the years, but, growing up with the two of them as my role models, I always knew what it meant to be a strong woman. Neither of them hesitated to share her opinion and fight for it to the end —for better or worse. I always knew I would not grow up to be someone's quiet, mousy wife.

And yet moving south seemed to transport us to something of a different time, a different mentality, in which women were so loyal to their husbands that it could blind them to everything else—and that's exactly what was happening with my mom. When Mitch was around, she was hushed, more reserved. She started letting him make all the decisions and was willing to go along with whatever he said or did, like he knew best about everything. Just like Mitch was the one to dictate where I could go and when and what kinds of clothes I could wear, he called the shots about what groceries the family could get, and he handled all the money. It was like he controlled the very concepts of what we wanted and needed. It never seemed like Mom was afraid of him— more like she was brainwashed by him, like her own opinions and needs were dulled.

And the influence of her friends and the church, who were largely tangled up into one entity, only further engrained that way of thinking. Just as I learned from our church that children should fall in line obediently behind their parents, the adults largely seemed to ascribe to the belief that women were to be silent and let the men speak and act for them. It's stated in the Baptist Faith and Message, the creed of the Southern Baptist Convention, that "a wife is to submit herself graciously to the servant leadership of her husband" and that she "has the God-given responsibility to respect her husband and to serve as his helper." It seemed Mom and Mitch came out of their Bible study classes as more and more of a single mind. It wasn't like they were in sync in some heartwarming, romantic way but like they couldn't function independently of one another, nor independently of the church. The family unit was supposed to fit into a neat and tidy package, nice and orderly, just like my mom always wanted. This belief system was one of the tools Mitch had wielded to manipulate us all and to make seemingly everyone around him believe that he had done nothing wrong. The church gave him the impression that he could do no wrong, and he stood firmly upon that platform to make Mom think that his desires and actions were not to be questioned, that she should support him and tell others to do the same. It was an expectation. Questioning any of it—what he had done, what they were covering up—would mean acknowledging flaws that she couldn't bear to face, let alone allow anyone else to see.

After they left that meeting with CPS, Nana said Mom was so angry that her legs were shaking.

A lawyer named Carol was then assigned by the court as my guardian ad litem—since I was a minor, she would be a legal advocate for me, helping to protect my interests as the investigation and trial moved forward. By court order, no one, not even Tommy, was supposed to discuss anything related to the case with me without first talking to Carol. Given the concerns expressed leading up to and during the meeting with CPS, Carol would be making visits to our apartment to check in on me and my well-being.

Even after she was back home in New York, Nana was like a liaison between Carol and me, continuing to speak up out of concern for me in ways I wasn't ready to do for myself. Once, when Carol hadn't heard back from me for a few days, she reached out to Nana to see if she had talked to me recently. Poor Nana told me later that her mind immediately jumped to some tragic outcome, that Mom had poisoned me or something. Actually, I had gone camping at a lake with the twins and their family and didn't have good cell phone reception. I hadn't given Nana or Carol a heads-up that I'd be away, but my mom could have told them. Then again, it's not like she and Nana were keeping each other up to date. Sometimes I felt like I might as well have been wearing one of those tracking ankle bracelets that parolees have to wear; my grandparents and Carol and Tommy and Laural all wanted tabs on me at all times.

I admit I *was* often ignoring Carol's calls. Tommy's, too. They were both showing up at my school a lot, the best place to get in touch with me without my mom interfering. As an adult, I get that they were doing their jobs, and I can't fault them—in fact, I credit them—for being so persistent, checking up on me and making sure they could get the information they needed. But as a teenager, I was mortified to get called to the SRO's office (the school resource officer, a cop assigned to the school) and to be seen talking with detectives and lawyers. Even if people didn't know who they were, their mere appearance stirred up questions and assumptions—Tommy with a police badge around his neck, Carol with her pantsuits and briefcase. I was never the type to break the rules, so whenever my name would be paged over the loudspeaker, a chorus of intrigued jabs would strike up from my peers: "Ooooh, you're in trouble!" Then the curiosity would grow to a swarm-like buzz surrounding me after the mysterious, important-looking people had said goodbye to me and walked out. That's not something you can easily create a cover story about and just brush off—in *any* scenario, and especially in a building filled with hundreds of nosy, gossipy teens. Everybody wanted to be in the know. It felt like Carol and Tommy were calling me constantly, asking me the same kinds of questions over and over. I'd already been through so many rounds of interviews. I was fed up.

Of course, ignoring their calls didn't actually help to calm anything down, but, in the moment, it felt good. To take some little action by not engaging. To make a choice.

After I got home from my trip, I did eventually catch up with Nana on the phone, and she then called Carol and told her I was home alone with no food, asking her to check on me. But Carol's visits were always by appointment, after having talked to Mom, who would then use that heads-up to make everything seem perfect, tidying up and stocking the kitchen with food that would later go to Mitch. She always bought a lot of fish, and he was the only one who liked seafood, so there was no questioning who that was for. And, of course, Mom was right by my side whenever I talked to Carol—affecting the image of a supportive, concerned mother but really only policing what I would say. It was all just more of the act.

Over time, my mother's methods of torment became more aggressive, and increasingly strange. If they hadn't happened to me directly, they might seem darkly comical, like snippets from a movie trailer about a woman gone mad, a maniacal religious fanatic—the viewer thinking that no one could *really* act this way. But she did. She threw holy water on me. When she first brought it into the room, I was afraid of what its powers might be. I made her touch it first, to know it wouldn't burn. She smacked me on the forehead, shouting, "Devil be gone!" She must have wanted so badly to erase what was happening that she thought she could cleanse it out of me. If only she could ever understand just how badly I wished the same thing for myself.

She once had a group of women pray over me while I was sleeping. I woke to the shadows of their looming figures, as if the room were closing in on me. There were movements and murmurings I couldn't quite pinpoint or make sense of. I was still groggy and thought maybe I was dreaming or having some sort of hallucination in my half-awake state. I thought maybe I had gone back in time, back to the abuse, or it had come back around to find me. There was the same rush of confusion, the same desire to push away while feeling frozen in place, as I tried to get my bearings. Four women I didn't recognize were standing around my bed, towering over me and chanting some sort of prayer. It was largely indistinguishable, but there were a lot of references to lying tongues. They wanted me to tell the truth.

A lot of the prayers I heard in those days were "for" me, as if they were generous favors from kind hearts. But in praying "for" me, my mother and her newfound, fanatical friends, who had become like Mitch's fan club, meant for me to awaken to the version of the world they kept insisting was real, one where Mitch was innocent and where I would come to my senses, admit that I'd made everything up, and thereby absolve my soul. They prayed for the truth to be revealed. And, of course, they prayed for Mitch as well. Perhaps we both needed some prayers—but their correlation was backward. They saw Mitch as the victim of *my* sins.

I did not, and will never, consider those prayers to be well intended. Misguided, maybe, at best. But such stubborn blindness is nothing but infuriating to me. They refused to hear me, to see me, as the broken child I was, pleading to be understood. The only brokenness they saw was a kind they thought they needed to fix, to scrub out. They weren't willing to believe they were aiming their scrub brushes at the wrong person.

By the time of the bedroom prayer intervention, that sort of lunacy had become the norm. Even as some part of me could identify it as crazy or scary, it was so common that I couldn't feel all that surprised.

And yet, when Tommy tried to question Mom about how I was being treated at home, she said, "I am offended that you would even think that I would have people in my home that would be hurting or upsetting my child."

After their little ritual was done, the women stayed at the apartment for a Bible study group. I walked past them through the living room on my way to the kitchen and could feel their eyes on me like laser pointers, tracking.

I didn't say anything—not then, and not even to Mom after they'd left. What was there to say? She wouldn't have an answer that would be at all logical or helpful anyway. As was the case in so many other elements of my life in those days, I resigned myself to just letting it all unfold around me and waiting. I was always waiting.

I was a child. I didn't know better. I didn't know anything different.

I floated through my days in a dissociative state, much like the one I'd learned so well during the abuse. I had to remain largely untethered from reality, because that escape was my only hope of holding onto my sanity.

The first couple of nights after Mitch had first been arrested—when I had just come home from Grandma Sally's, Mom just back from her trip to Africa, both of us worn out from our conversations at the police station—I slept next to Mom in her bed, hoping to find some little crevice of comfort. I don't know why I thought I would find it there. She had been so cold to me ever since arriving back home and cracking open this terrible subject that now lay between us. Maybe I was still searching for the warmth I had been hoping for all those years before, waiting for her to turn to me and let her walls down, saying, "I'm so sorry. I'm here for you. I believe you."

Instead, she started putting up more and more pictures of

Mitch throughout her bedroom, as if she were holding a vigil in his memory. I guess she kind of was, as she continued to pray for him to come home. But this was no missing-person or prisoner-of-war case; he was a criminal, an abuser, a rapist—and she wanted him there next to her, instead of me.

So, I was forced out of that attempted place of refuge and had to try to learn to sleep on my own again. It was odd to find myself missing sleeping in their room; for so long, it had been a source of trauma and anxiety but also something I had perceived as a source of comfort. In a vicious cycle, my fear of being alone only escalated the longer the abuse went on. I had turned to Mitch and my mother again and again over the years, never fully wanting to accept that neither of them would ever be there for me in the right ways.

I told Nana about the pictures and how much they were freaking me out. She tried asking Mom about them on my behalf. Mom said, "You gotta remember, that's Caleb's father."

Because their relationship was the one that mattered. The one that wasn't yet shattered beyond repair. Maybe if she kept her energy invested in salvaging that, she could keep the ratty bow tied tight around her family image.

Clearly, the photo-memorial approach did resonate with Caleb in some way, as soon he also plastered pictures of Mitch all over his bedroom door. Now my other former hideout was lost to me, as well. The apartment felt like it was shrinking, closing in around me, as the pictures spread like a rash and forced me to think of Mitch at every turn. I always felt like he was looking at me, watching me. Even in his absence, I was surrounded by him.

One morning, I walked out of my bedroom to be greeted by blown-up pictures of him and Bible verses—more attempts to shame me into thinking I needed absolution—taped to the walls throughout the living room. Mitch's face was several feet tall; his huge eyes seemed to follow me from all sides, as words from the Scriptures screamed at me from the towering, handwritten signs, as if waved at me by protestors.

John 8:32 (CSB): "The truth will set you free."

James 1:26 (CSB): "If anyone thinks he is religious without controlling his tongue, his religion is useless and he deceives himself."

1 Peter 3:10 (CSB): "For the one who wants to love life and to see good days, let him keep his tongue from evil and his lips from speaking deceit."

It was dizzying just to try to get my bearings and walk across the floor; Mitch often leered at me in my dreams, and now the nightmares were staring me down, making me question whether I was really awake.

The posters stayed up for weeks, maybe months. Mom sure was quick to take them down any time Carol or a CPS officer was coming over, though.

To say I was lying would be a lie in and of itself. I *had* told the truth, but it was one they didn't like. They wanted to shame me into coming out with a different version of things, a pretend one that they would dress up as truth. It had taken so much courage and pain to finally tell the truth I had been hiding for so long, and now I was only being punished further for it. It was so confusing.

And it was all so hypocritical; *they* were the liars. I wished they would read those verses with a critical lens aimed at themselves instead of me, that they would take an honest look at their own sins. But their thinking has remained backwards all these years. Long after Mitch's conviction, I received Facebook messages from Barb, Mom's friend with all the car-ride criticisms, telling me it's never too late to change course and make the choices God wants me to make. Even after I responded to say that I'm right where God intended me to be and that she was the one who supported a child molester and a woman who abandoned her daughter, Barb called my mom and Mitch wonderful people who were "thriving" and dismissed my words as having parted ways with reality.

With my mother brazenly at the helm, that group has remained focused on preserving their image; they are stubborn in their charade of being thoroughly good-hearted people, doing what the Lord would want them to do. That charade depended upon knocking me down and keeping me there. They were willing to sacrifice me for their own benefit. None of that seems very Christian to me.

New Girl in an Old Town

Evidently, having Mitch across the street wasn't close enough for my mother; in addition to visiting him regularly, she wanted to have him over to our place—which, of course, couldn't happen with me around. I felt like I was in the way while in my own home. So, in the summer after my junior year of high school, I went to New York to stay with Nana and Poppy again, to get some much-needed distance from the turmoil my daily life had become.

They got on the road to come pick me up after having both worked all day. Never one to be accommodating, Mom told them if they couldn't get there by eight the next morning, they'd have to wait until the evening to pick me up, because Caleb had an away game for baseball and we'd be gone all day. I certainly would have been happy to skip the game and just wait at the apartment for them to arrive, but that wasn't an option Mom was willing to consider. So, desperate to do whatever was needed to get me out of there, Nana and Poppy drove the twelve hours straight through, stopping in a parking lot to sleep for just an hour or two. They loaded my bags into their car in the early-morning light and wasted no time for fake pleasantries with my mother. Exhausted as they must have been, they turned right back in the direction they'd just come from and headed back to New York. That long stretch of I-71 had come to feel like an escape route, a well-worn one whose traffic patterns made familiar bumps and sways as I slept against the window.

My visits in New York were quiet, low-key, exactly as I needed them to be. That was the summer my grandparents got Bella, knowing how much I loved dogs. She quickly became "mine," following me everywhere and snuggling up with me on the couch and in bed all night. Poppy worked from home, and it was nice to be able to exchange a joke with him in passing or make sandwiches together for lunch. Nana would take me shopping for school clothes and ask me to be her sidekick when running errands. Sometimes we'd all go see a movie or spend a hot day at a water park. Most week-nights, we settled in together to watch *Wheel of Fortune* and *Jeopardy*, shouting out the answers and laughing as we stumbled over our words in our excitement. I could laugh there. I could breathe.

I was planning to go back to Tennessee for school that fall, to try to enjoy my senior year with my friends and favorite teachers, my final cheerleading and dance team seasons, to attend my prom, have fancy portraits taken for the yearbook. Mom decided she wanted Mitch to stay with her instead. I had been sent on a one-way trip to New York without notice.

My mother had cast me out like an employee who's fired, effective immediately, and sent out the door with a single box to hold her belongings. I had left home with a suitcase—one suitcase, as if I were going on a week-long vacation.

I would have used that suitcase space so much differently

if I had known, if I had been granted the time to prepare. I would have said goodbyes that weren't just fleeting *see you laters*; I would have kept my friends by my side while packing, all the way up to the moment I closed the car door, after long hugs goodbye, savoring their presence without assuming we would just pick up our usual routines in a few weeks. This was not just a new chapter, but an entirely new edition. In a different language. With no one to translate.

Mom got what she wanted: now she had her neat and tidy family unit, with her husband and their child, all together in one place and pretending like everything was fine. She had removed me from the equation, an obstacle she was sick of stumbling over, and now she could polish up the image she wanted so badly to portray to everyone around her.

She sent me a few boxes of my things, but it was all random junk I wasn't likely to use: half-empty hair products, old curling irons I'd stopped using a long time ago, a few little decorations from my room. Not the ones I would have chosen. There was none of the practical stuff that I really needed: no clothes, no dance shoes, nothing that would have helped me keep good memories close.

The few things that had been getting me through each day in Tennessee—my friends, dance and cheerleading, the simple familiarity of my daily routines—were now robbed from me as well. Despite the comforts of being with my grandparents, the shock of this news and the changes it spilled out before me left me feeling thrown out into the cold without a jacket. I was untethered, off balance.

Still, in many ways, I'd become accustomed to adapting as life-changing jolts were thrown at me. *It's okay,* I'd reassure myself. *I've got this.* I'd analyze what the new norms and rules were, what would get me in trouble versus what might help things stay calm, what obstacles I needed to dodge. It had become an instinct of sorts: how to operate within parameters that seemed to change constantly. But it wasn't a skill I'd wanted to develop. I'd been trying for years to keep it together just a little bit longer. This latest turn felt like the darkest one yet—and one there was no coming back from. A door had been closed behind me. By finally taking the steps to shed the layer of my life I could no longer endure, I was forced to leave behind the entire life I had known.

Earlier in the summer—when I'd thought I was just visiting—Nana had made a couple of appointments for me with a social worker, Debbie, whom she'd been going to counseling sessions with and really liked. Given the struggles I'd had in trying to connect with counselors in Tennessee, I was hesitant. In fact, I was still pretty closed off to the whole idea.

"I don't need to talk to a therapist. I'm not crazy!" I told Nana—and myself.

The truth was that I was scared to talk to anyone else about what I'd been through. Talking about it only made me relive it, only made it all feel even more real and present, like something I hadn't yet escaped from. It seemed like all I'd been doing for months was telling an endless line of professionals the same details over and over again. I didn't know how much more of it I was willing to take on, didn't know if I could make myself open that door even one more time.

But then I met Debbie.

I went to the first appointment reluctantly, figuring I owed it to Nana to at least give it a try, even if a halfhearted attempt was the best I could manage. Nana stayed with me for the first session. I felt both embarrassed that I needed her there and infinitely safer by having her next to me. I didn't know if I could find any words to share yet, if I could bring anything more to the surface. Nana spoke for me, laying out the details of what Mitch had done to me, of what my mom and her church friends were doing to me. Hearing it second-hand was almost just as painful, but at least I could sit there in the cocoon of my silence while the words washed over us. Nana was animated by the release of information: loud, angry, pleading, relieved of some of the burden. She shouted, she cursed, she cried. She and I were often opposite extremes like that: I couldn't let myself tap into my emotions, while Nana's filled the small room to the point where it felt like the walls wouldn't hold.

Despite my silence, I sensed there was something different about this place, this person. Debbie's office had a warm glow, with décor like something straight out of a Pinterest post I would have pinned. The low white couch was actually comfortable and cute instead of an institutional, cold leather; I sank into it, hugged by blue, fringed throw pillows. The lighting was soft, instantly relaxing me, just bright enough to highlight the inspirational quotes and knick-knacks scattered tastefully around the room. A sound machine whirred softly in the corner, which helped me to feel like people walking by in the hall wouldn't hear what we were saying, and a soothing scent—lavender?—surrounded me. I glanced around for a candle or diffuser, but its source must have been tucked away somewhere out of sight. I felt like I was in her living room rather than a tiny corner of an office complex. As Debbie talked softly, maintaining eye contact and nodding in response to Nana's outpourings, I could tell that the atmosphere reflected her personality: inviting, reassuring. I felt something opening up inside myself, calling out for me to listen and trust it. *Not yet*, I thought. But knowing it was there, that I might be ready to turn to it soon, was some sort of reassurance.

Being told unceremoniously that I would be staying in New York presented both a need to work through even more trauma and an opportunity to continue working with Debbie. So, I agreed to go to more appointments with her—largely by force of circumstance, but also with a curiosity to see if I could let that little inner voice start to speak up.

It took me a long time to say much of anything in our sessions. Talking about the abuse remained very difficult for me, and now the grief of missing my friends engulfed me and made it even harder to sort out what I was feeling, let alone express it to someone else. To her immense credit, Debbie didn't push me. She could tell where I was and wasn't ready to go—so we started small.

"Sometimes we can't access feelings," she said, in a tone that told me she'd seen this countless times. It made me feel less alone. "So, let's just try to get some facts."

She would ask me about my mom, my brother, my friends. Like she wanted to know about them, who they were, before we got to how gutted I was without them in my life. She would ask me about school, about church, about growing up in Westbridge and moving to Tennessee and what I liked about each place. She would ask me about positive things about my relationship with Mitch: how much he had helped in raising me, how he made me laugh. It felt safer to acknowledge the good things.

I could talk about those things, at least in little snippets. My voice often felt even quieter than it usually is, as if I had a cold and couldn't quite get a full breath. But I could push through it. I could even talk about some of the bad stuff when it was fact-based; I'd had a lot of practice doing that already, and Nana had laid a lot of that groundwork in our first session. I could reiterate, confirm, string together some facts into sentences. The whats and whens and wheres. Some of the hows.

But not the whys. And not how I felt, at least not the terrible depths of it, the bottomlessness. And not what had been done to me as the sum total of all those smaller facts.

Whenever we would try to shift into emotions, or details tied too closely to emotions, I often couldn't bring up any words. Maybe some yesses and nos. There was a lot of not remembering. A lot of "I don't know."

Debbie would try to guide me: "If you had to guess..."

But still I couldn't come up with much of anything to say. It was like searching in a dark room without a flashlight. I wasn't sure what was in there and wasn't sure I really wanted to see it.

Sometimes it's easier to stay in the dark.

Sometimes I could feel my eyes glaze over and was aware of my mind going black, like watching the sunset dip below the horizon or feeling your thoughts become blurry and strange as you start to fall asleep.

Sometimes I didn't know where I went. I'd just be gone for a little while.

This was when I first learned the term "dissociating." Debbie explained to me that this was something I'd learned by necessity during the abuse: Mitch was having sex with my body, but my mind was up in the ceiling somewhere. That disconnect can be so essential to surviving trauma that it simply takes over, automatically, and it continued to do so for me even that long after the truth had come to light and the immediate abuse had stopped. I was still living through the ramifications of the abuse, and now new forms of it from my mother, and so the dissociating also continued. Sometimes it still does today.

Debbie was always so gentle, so patient. She'd talk through the simpler stuff—what I liked to do with my friends, my favorite stores to shop at—as if we had all the time in the world, as if we were just two girlfriends catching up. Then she'd say, almost apologetically, like a nurse giving a shot and warning you that it might sting a bit, "You know, eventually we have to talk about what happened with Mitch. With your mom."

She taught me some mindfulness techniques to try to help ground me before forging into emotional territory. With my feet planted on the floor, hands in my lap, breathing slowly and deeply, we'd talk through objective facts about our current surroundings: "The color of the wall is salmon. There are pictures hanging on the wall. There's an air vent in the corner." These simple, objective statements were supposed to help prepare my mind for the transition into the more complicated stuff, but I would easily get distracted by what was coming next, upset by it before it arrived. The questions I knew she'd soon have to ask were monsters lurking outside the door, and I didn't want her to let them in.

Debbie encouraged me to do the mindfulness work at home, too, whenever I started feeling anxious or depressed, but it felt like homework, and I often didn't have the motivation to follow through, or I'd too easily doubt that I'd be able to handle it on my own. Instead, I continued to dissociate, to block things out, and to float through many of those days in a numb and distracted state.

Any attempt at conversation—from Debbie or from my grandparents—about Mom not letting me come back absolutely shut me down. It was like I could feel my brain saying, *Nope. Can't do it.* I couldn't comprehend not going back to my room, my things, my friends and classmates and church group, my brother. After everything I'd been through, and with all that we were still working our way through, how could my mom deny me that? Did she not want me?

Debbie could talk me out of the darkness unlike anyone else, even more than Nana and Poppy, despite knowing me for so much less time. She was removed enough from the situation to be an objective observer, while also having the expertise and compassion to understand all that I was dealing with, deep down to the core of it, to describe and analyze it in ways I couldn't yet. She talked to me like I was my own person and could make my own choices.

The conviction with which she told me "*You* have control of your life" was fascinating to me—so unfamiliar, so appealing. As I gradually started opening up more over the course of our first several months of sessions, I realized I didn't have to think about what she would *want* me to say or how what I said would affect other people. I could just tell her the truth, plain and simple: exactly what I was feeling in that moment, what was keeping me up at night, what I questioned about myself and my future. I never once felt like she was judging me or critiquing me in her head, the way I did with most other people.

I struggled to find anything remotely close to that level of trust with friends. New York had been my childhood home but had been left in the rearview mirror long ago, and life there had continued without me. Tennessee was more familiar, was where I'd spent my formative preteen-to-teenage years, and, most importantly, was where my friends were. And in your early teens, of course, your friends are like something even more than family. They're how you define yourself, how you understand yourself, how you feel guided and grounded and whole. My friends didn't see me as a rape victim or a sinner; they saw me as a shy but kindhearted girl, fiercely loyal, laughing together as we danced around my room. Now, *they* were what I'd left behind, and without warning. I was back where I'd started, but the entire landscape was different now, and I was different within it.

In many ways, I wasn't so much starting over in a new town but *re*starting in my *old* town. Since we hadn't moved to Tennessee until the summer after I finished fifth grade, many of my New York peers remembered me from elementary school, which invited even more curiosity and questions: why I left, why I came back, why I came back with just one year left of school. I admit I would have had those same questions if I were on the other side of the conversation. But I walked around with a constant tension in my spine, an incessant inner mantra of *Please don't ask me. Please don't ask me.*

One of the most common questions was also one of the most dreaded, as it was particularly knotted up with my painful past: the change in my last name. These people had known me before the adoption. I reappeared after a six-year absence looking strikingly familiar but with a different name. Explaining any of that inevitably meant mentioning Mitch, which always meant coming dangerously close to having to unveil my whole story. I kept all of my answers as short as possible, which, I'm sure, only added to people's curiosity and speculation. As for the weirdness of showing up back in town just for senior year, I told people I'd come back to help take care of my grandparents—always with a slight pang in my core, knowing the reverse was true.

There was no hiding, either—Westbridge was a much smaller school than the one I'd gone to in Tennessee, Green Valley. I graduated with about 180 students, whereas in Tennessee each class had more than 400. The freshman wing of Green Valley was the size of the entire Westbridge high school. Everyone knew I was "the new girl," knew about my impending arrival before it happened. At Green Valley, you met someone new in each class period! There would have been names called at that graduation, members of my own class, whom I'd never met, probably some names I'd never even heard. At Westbridge, everyone knew everyone. And we sort of knew each other from when I'd lived there before, but not really, not anymore. I'd left these people as children and circled back to them as young adults. We knew something of each other and yet were strangers. In the years I'd been gone, they'd formed, broken, and shifted so many friendships and relationships that I'd never be able to catch up.

Being the new kid in town is always hard. Tack onto that being the kid who's years behind on what everyone else knows *and* being the kid who everyone else *thinks* they know all about, all while carrying the darkness of years of trauma, and it feels impossible.

Cheerleading was my safety net, which I clung to pretty desperately at times. It was something I had always been passionate about in Tennessee and was how I had made some of my closest friends there. By the time I had arrived in Westbridge that summer, the squad was already practicing, having held tryouts back in the spring. I figured I had missed my chance. Luckily, though, my uncle was the head football coach, and he talked to the cheerleading coach about me. Given my background in both cheer and dance, he assured her I could catch up quickly and asked if there were any spots open. Luck was on my side again in that two people had recently quit, so I was given the opportunity to try out for one of those spots.

I tried to convey confidence through my smile as I performed my toe touches and the assigned cheer to the table full of people watching, evaluating. I wanted—needed—to be let into this hub that I hoped would feel somewhat familiar, to give me something known amidst so much upheaval. *Please like me*, my mind thrummed as a surge of adrenaline propelled me through the routine. *Please let me have this.*

I made the squad, and a foreign exchange student named Sophie who had tried out alongside me took the other spot. She was from Germany, tall and blonde, with a heavy accent and a sweet, open demeanor. It was comforting to meet someone else right away who was also navigating new territory. It was a natural foundation for a friendship, one that carried us through our senior year together. I was grateful to feel a little less alone.

Other than cheerleading practice and counseling, though, I barely left the house that summer, barely even left my bedroom. Other girls from the squad would invite me out, but I would feel a sharp tug of suspicion in my gut and think, *They're not my friends*. My mind raced through all the possibilities of what they might say to me or ask me about, what they'd be thinking as I spoke or would say to each other after I left, what their hidden intentions might be in wanting to spend time with me. The entire concept of trust had been obliterated from my mind; it simply didn't exist anymore. I couldn't make sense of the idea of being open and honest with people, of the expectation that a person could be honest with *me*, or be loyal, or have my best interests at heart.

By the time the school year had started, that discomfort was part of my everyday attire. While Green Valley's atmosphere had been very high energy and supportive—with everybody involved in something, pep rallies every Friday, a celebratory family—it felt at Westbridge like everybody hated each other. A negative, distrusting attitude permeated the halls. Senior year in Tennessee would have been such a different experience.

The hardest part was lunchtime. I didn't know anyone well enough to sit with and didn't want to be seen sitting in the corner by myself. The self-consciousness ingrained in me by my mother surrounded me everywhere, like a physical barrier that kept others from getting too close to me and didn't let me take the risk of approaching them. So, for the first couple weeks, I spent the lunch period in the bathroom, just waiting it out. Skipping a meal has never been a big deal to me, and by that time I was certainly accustomed to it. My friends in Tennessee had lunch around the same time, so we'd call each other or text, which made the time pass quickly —I could never get enough of that connection to the familiar comforts of my previous life—and yet it made them feel even farther away. Their lives were moving on without me there.

Soon, though, even that shoddy cocoon I'd created for myself was unraveled. A teacher found out that I'd been waiting lunch out in the bathroom and told me I couldn't be in there. In Tennessee, where the campus was like its own village, with multiple buildings and outdoor courtyards to cross to get from one subject's wing to another, we wandered wherever we wanted during lunch: roaming the halls, going to our lockers, heading to our next classroom early to catch up with friends before class started. But, evidently, the West-bridge staff wanted us to stay in the cafeteria until the bell rang. I didn't even realize I'd been breaking the rules! I just wanted a little window of escape. Thankfully, I soon discovered that Sophie had the same lunch period as I did, so I sat with her, grateful to have a partner in navigating that intimidating scene.

While it seemed like everyone else's senior year was easy, their schedules filled in haphazardly with fun or blow-off classes, mine was packed with classes I would need to pass in order to graduate, including some I'd already taken in

Tennessee for which the credits didn't transfer. I'd taken algebra my freshman year and had since taken Advanced Placement classes, but because New York State has its own standardized exams required for graduation, all of that work was wasted, and I found myself starting over in yet another way. It felt like I was cramming a whole four-year course load into that one year.

I didn't even know whether I was going to graduate until a few days before the ceremony because of those exams. I'd become quite familiar with pushing through stress, but that added source of it was the last thing I needed. I often felt like my head and heart were stretched to max capacity, staggering step by step under the weight of all they were carrying. Then something else would get piled on, and I would recalibrate, pushing things down to make room and assessing *this* as the new normal to operate under. Once again, I was telling myself, *I'm fine, I'm fine, I'm fine,* hoping that thinking it persistently enough would will it to be true.

Throughout all of that stress at school, I was also flying back to Tennessee a lot for court dates and meetings in preparation for *more* court dates. I always wondered what my classmates thought about my frequent trips out of state. If anyone asked, I'd say something vague about visiting family. Maybe my peers thought I was homesick, running back to where I'd come from any chance I could get. I *was* always a little bit homesick, in both states. I felt very much divided between the two places, never fully settled or at home in either. The bad things about Tennessee still had their claws in me, while the good ones were slipping too far away to hold onto. And New York's familiarity was too long gone to provide comfort. I still felt like a visitor and wondered if that would ever change, the worry a deep ache I carried with me everywhere.

I'm still not sure if the move to New York was what was

best for me. In many ways it helped, of course—getting me away from Mitch, from the constant reminders of what he'd done to me, and from my mother and her church squad. But, in just as many ways, it was its own kind of trauma. The fact that I, a rape victim, spent the first many weeks of my counseling sessions focusing instead on this—*I miss my friends; what am I doing here; how could my mom do this to me; why doesn't she want me there?*—provides evidence I can't ignore about how deeply it had rattled me. And it felt harder to hide in New York, harder to blend into the background, not just at school, but everywhere. I was used to hiding in Tennessee, slinking through my days without raising alarm bells. I was good at it. In Westbridge, the town and the stores and the school were so small, and I was a sudden transplant. Glaringly obvious, like when you're walking down a quiet hallway and your shoes are squeaking against the tiles. Exposed. I was surrounded by different kinds of reminders of my family and what had happened to us, reminders of the mother I no longer had in my life. A lot of our relatives still lived in or near the same small rural county, so I never knew when I'd cross paths with someone who knew me—and have to wonder just how much they knew: which version of me? Whose version of the truth?

Nana has always said my mom uses her phone as a weapon, and that's exactly what she'd done in the early days after my relocation, rushing to get in touch with as many connections in New York as she could, making sure they heard her version of events before having the chance to speak with me directly and perhaps make a genuine connection. She made sure to intercept, to get the word out that I was a liar, to protect herself and Mitch against whatever I might say. And the word did get out, quickly—people in small towns talk.

Before I was even given a chance to speak for myself, or to choose to keep things quiet, everyone had already heard my mom's revision of my story. She would tell people maybe one percent of what had unfolded over hours of courtroom testimony, a heavily edited highlight reel that took some things out of context, eliminated others, and skewed the entire story. And then those people, either unaware of or unconcerned about Mom's bias, would continue to spread that narrative, the misinformation and blatant lies rippling out far beyond my reach. There was no way for me to tell my own story on my own time.

Once, I ran into a friend of Mom's in the waiting room at Debbie's office. Evidently, she was a patient of another therapist there. The space between us after that initial moment of eye contact and recognition was electric with a mutual recoil. I could tell there were questions sprinting through her head that she couldn't decide whether to ask, and I wished I could disappear. I hated feeling like I had to hide everywhere I went—and, worse, that I *couldn't* hide, no matter how badly I might want to. After that, Debbie and the other therapist were careful to coordinate their schedules so that we wouldn't overlap again. I appreciated it, even if it made me feel a bit like the problem child who has to be seated proactively at a fancy event.

The one that hurt the most, though, was my cousin Kristin. Technically speaking, in terms of genealogy, we're some sort of distant cousins: her dad is my mom's second cousin once removed. I'm not even sure what that makes us. But that never dictated our emotional closeness, which was more akin to the kind of friendship that feels like sisterhood. We're the same age—only a couple weeks apart—and went to the same school. She was a built-in friend, the kind you're given from birth. When I'd lived in New York as a kid, the two of us and our moms hung out all the time. Those are some of my favorite memories from my childhood: the shopping trips the four of us would take every couple weeks, sauntering through the mall with bags loaded with clothes and fun accessories, Kristin and me obsessed with dolphin jewelry and sequined purses, always finishing the day with root beers from the Arby's drive-thru. I still hold those memories close. Despite good intentions, Kristin and I had largely lost touch after I'd moved to Tennessee. There was no falling out, just a slow drift, our communication less and less frequent until it came to consist just of occasional texts or liking of each other's Facebook posts. Being back offered us an opportunity to reconnect. I was grateful for a familiar face to turn to and hoped we could pick things up where they'd left off. That things could be like they used to be.

But nothing was like it used to be.

Kristin's mom was one of the people my mom had called to get into her pocket. That part didn't surprise me. What did surprise me was how completely the poison had trickled down to Kristin herself, how easily she'd been convinced I was a liar, that I was the one to be distrusted and shunned. I guess I'd been gone too long.

Kristin's betrayal was largely the passive-aggressive kind. She wouldn't say things to me outright but would say them to others just before I entered the room or just after I'd left, amplifying the stares I always suspected were on me and creating a ripple of whispers everywhere I went. People knew about our relationship, how close we used to be, and that she had inside connections with my family, so I suspect they sought her out for the latest details, and she certainly didn't hesitate to distribute them. She seemed a little more daring on Facebook. Even though she knew (and probably hoped) I'd be likely to see her posts, that little bit of distance, the seeming protection of hiding behind a screen, emboldened her to say more. "Supporting my Uncle Mitch today," she captioned a selfie in a white T-shirt—a symbol of innocence that Mitch's team of supporters adopted—the "uncle" a strange way to put it, as they had no such relationship in terms of genealogy nor any sort of close bond. I wouldn't even have thought she'd remember Mitch well, from their limited interactions when we were kids. Mitch might have said a brief hello to her before we ladies piled into the car to go out and about for the afternoon. He was on the outskirts; I was the one she was supposed to know well. But, of course, my mom had also been an integral part of our shared past, and now Kristin had jumped readily onto that team, her white shirt screaming out from my phone screen in its stark allegiance with those fighting against me.

So, having moved to New York, even hundreds of miles away, even with my mother having cut herself out of my life like a photo after a breakup, I couldn't escape her presence. She remained with me in all the ways I didn't want and left me longing for the rest.

Somehow, I made it through those difficult final months of high school. I put most of what energy I had into cheerleading. Sometimes the painted-on smiles and choreographed enthusiasm felt real. I dated a few guys—most of them briefly, casually, without telling them about my past. I largely stayed holed up in my room, snuggling with Bella and blasting Taylor Swift as I studied her posters plastered all over my walls. I passed my exams and graduated. I started taking gen-ed classes at a nearby community college.

Even there, the details of the surroundings were new, but

they felt far too similar. Any time someone struck up a conversation with me, I watched their eyes watching me, studying me, and heard criticisms and mocking questions running through their heads as if they were shouting them at me or, worse, whispering them tauntingly in my ear. Girls especially. I assumed they were all gossiping about me, acting like they'd be my friend just to get dirt about what had happened to me and report back to the others.

With each step, my past continued to define my future. Step by incremental step, I pushed on to move forward as best I could, but never without keeping careful watch over my shoulder.

After we graduated high school, Kristin and I ended up working at the same company, a large office filled with cubicles, where I sat for eight hours a day staring at invoices and spreadsheets.

I realized too late that Kristin had forced her way back into my life only to mess with me. Her turning against me, which had initially been such a disorienting shock to my system during our senior year, soon grew into what I could only see as a calculated plot against me. She was like an undercover spy, infiltrating, and she was thorough in her work.

We were on different teams, thankfully, so our jobs didn't force us to interact, but my desk was in her direct line of sight, so I quite literally always felt her watching me. My clothes, my phone conversations, my casual chit-chat with coworkers around me, my level of attention or distraction, my coffee or lunch or lack thereof—I felt like it was all being documented, compiled into a big file that could be referenced and used against me at any time, reported back to my mom. I had finally started to let my guard down enough to make friends with a few girls there, whom I'd chat with on breaks or order takeout with for lunch—friends who proved trustworthy throughout my ordeal and who I'm thankful to still have close to me today. But even when I was with them around the office, I was always a bit distracted, a jumpiness in my spine as I anticipated Kristin's approach. It was like I was never free to be myself or to try to figure out what an independent life as a young adult might look like for me.

This all proved to be merely a warm-up act, building up to her greatest affront against me, a punch that wouldn't land until a few years later—long after Mitch had gone to prison and I'd been working hard to hold onto some sense of closure.

As if our constant orbit in the office throughout those years wasn't enough, Kristin then welcomed herself into the circle of my closest friends, a group my then-boyfriend and I had been hanging out with regularly for several years. We were an established unit, intricately interwoven, worn in comfortably like a favorite pair of jeans, and suddenly Kristin was there, so glaringly out of place that it was a constant distraction, an irritation. She was an extra puzzle piece, trying to force the fit. I couldn't understand how the others didn't see it.

Especially Joe. He was one of the people in the group I'd grown closest to; he was my boyfriend's best friend, and the three of us hung out practically every day, whether on our own or in bigger groups. We'd go out for dinner or drinks, or hang out at each other's houses and talk for hours. Kristin was well aware of Joe's frequent presence in my life. And I'm pretty sure that's exactly why she decided she needed to date him. As a jab at me. A way to keep even closer tabs on me and worm her way deeper under my skin. She latched onto him quickly—*weirdly* quickly—thereby also becoming a near-daily presence.

Just like when we were in high school, Kristin would plant herself into a conversation, say something weighted, and watch for any twitch of reaction from me: "It's not nice to lie, you know." Having her around was like having my mother or the church ladies in the room; she was like a parrot trained by them, swooping in to observe, to squawk out something irritating, and to take back to them what she'd attained. There were so many little looks and comments, played just subtly enough that the others might not pick up on them but that I felt very strongly. It was more of the same petty, angsty games; she refused to grow up and move on.

I tried opening up to Joe and the others about it. They'd known me long enough and well enough to know the truth about my past and all that I still carried from it. They'd been in my life during my multiple trips to Tennessee, including the two-week trial; they knew that Mitch was in prison. They had seemed to believe me. So, I thought I could count on them to listen—to *hear* me, to side with me—when I confided in them about this latest battle. When I told them that this girl I'd known so much longer than any of them couldn't be trusted. When I asked them not to bring her deeper into my life, to help keep some distance. "I really don't want to be around her," I'd say. "If she's gonna show up, let me know so I don't show up."

I remember those conversations well, because they weren't easy for me. I'm not the most assertive person, but I knew I needed to be adamant here: "I don't want what I do with my life to get back to my mom and Mitch." *My* life. I was working so hard to stake a claim, to make my life be my own. I wanted to be able to go out and have a few drinks

150

without being distracted by the thought of Kristin reporting back, "She got *so* drunk. She's an alcoholic."

They all—Joe, especially—seemed to understand, to agree to help me set those boundaries.

I don't know what Kristin was saying to them, but somehow she must have been more convincing. She continued to show up everywhere. It was unnerving, knowing she could pop up at any moment; I could no longer relax around my own friends. And now my group of once-trusted confidants had been contaminated by the same types of looks and whispers that used to surround me in high school. I always felt like I'd walked in right after she'd said something terrible about me, leading the others to second-guess me and assess me with questions in their eyes. It was the full-body kind of uncomfortable, every part of me antsy, crawling with awkwardness, wishing I could run out of the room but not wanting to call any more attention to myself.

As the tension between us grew more and more palpable among the group, the others started telling *me* to be nice to *her*. It was the strangest switch, this role-swapping; it jolted me. It stung. Sure, it would have been easier on everyone if things could have just been calm and carefree, but how could they not have seen that no one wanted that—*needed* that—more than me? After all that I'd been through? Calm and carefree was what I craved every day, but it remained out of reach. They were keeping it out of reach. I couldn't under-stand their thought process. Kristin was supporting the person who had hurt me—the *people* who *continued* to hurt me. And in doing so, she was one of them. How do you tell a victim to be nice to her abusers?

And then it hit me: I'd seen this before. I knew this pain all too well—the face-slap of victim shaming. Just like too many others before them had done, they were making *me* feel

151

guilty and apologetic for things that had been done to me. As if I didn't already wish I could erase it all; as if it weren't enough to wish the abuse wasn't a part of *my* life. Now I was supposed to feel bad about making it a part of theirs? I had thought I was safe with them, that they could be a refuge for me to forget all that was bad in my life and get to enjoy being an easygoing young adult. That I could finally relax, could finally fit in.

To lose that outlet, and to have my trust betrayed once again, made me feel like I was losing my mind. I was at a loss as to how to handle it. This kind of pain burned in a different way, coursing throughout my body, waking me up at night, leaving me on edge and distracted. Now I wasn't just hurt, but *angry*. Angry that Kristin continued to be welcomed into the group when they all knew she didn't support me. Particularly angry at Joe for pursuing that relationship when he'd known the truth of my situation for years. And angry that, in dismissing my concerns, they had dragged me backward on my road to recovery. They were allowing me to be put right back into a situation I had worked hard to distance myself from for years. A knife had been driven deep into my back, and I felt it with me everywhere I went. There was no dislodging it.

In my disappointment with them, I had started pushing each of these false friends away, and before long I knew I needed to push *myself* away, to remove myself from the entire situation—not just Kristin, but the rest of the group, soon including my boyfriend too. We'd held on a bit longer than the rest, but his continued connection to the group after I'd left it stretched our tether to the point of fraying and then snapping. Seeing Instagram posts of him with Kristin and the others, grinning at parties, clustered together like pieces forming a whole, made the juxtaposition of our paths too clear to ignore: his and theirs moving forward as if all was right with the world while mine felt at times stuck in place and at others careening backward. It had become clear that it was all or nothing: accept Kristin in the group or refuse to be a part of it myself. I was infuriated that they'd left me with that ultimatum, but I couldn't fight against it anymore. It was like the burnt popcorn smell again: nauseating, suffocating. I couldn't stand to be around it for another minute.

I no longer have any sort of relationship with any of them —and now I know that if that's the kind of energy they were going to contribute to my life, I'm better off without them. But it was hard to convince myself of that at the time. And it was hard to find any sort of empowerment in walking away, because it didn't feel like a choice I was making but, rather, yet another choice that had been made for me, forced upon me. Like dominoes clattering down, the loss of my friendship with Kristin took several others out with it, ones I had thought were strong enough to withstand her manipulation. I continued to experience ripples of betrayal, aftershocks from Mitch's actions—the choices he made years ago now trickling all the way down to my once-trustworthy group of friends in a small town eight hundred miles away from where he sat in his prison cell.

As my social life was collapsing and I retreated further and further inward, I still had to go to work and try to trudge through the nine-to-five. I shuffled around with blinders up as much as I could, envisioning myself in a bubble to insulate myself and keep my surroundings at a safe distance. But being at the office meant being around Kristin, and soon my bubble began to feel increasingly opaque, by necessity, darker and smaller, not as much a bubble as a box. The box was closing in on me, and I couldn't get away from it. I would sit at my desk all day and only think about Mitch and what he'd done to me, about all that he had taken from me.

This is why I say moving back to New York may not have been the best thing for me. In this way, in fact, it was very, very bad for me. In this way, it was like I'd never left Tennessee, never broken free from the abuse. It had followed me. And I feared it would always follow me.

A Victim on Trial

THE CIRCUS CONTINUED AS COURT DATES BEGAN FOR THE trial, the culmination that four years of interviews, investigation, and hearings had been leading up to—"big-boy court," as Tommy called it. So much of it played out like a disorienting dream, where you're pretty sure it's not real, but you're not able to take control of it and turn it into something that makes sense.

My senses were both dulled and heightened by the August Tennessee heat that permeated the courtroom like fog, the air conditioner broken. At least I could blame the sweat and the need for deep breaths on that rather than nerves. The judge kept apologizing to all of us; he was assured it would be fixed soon, and thus tried to assure us of the same, but our collective confidences in that promise dwindled with each passing day of humidity and sticky skin against wooden seats.

In addition to Laural and Tommy, I had Nana and Poppy there to support me throughout the trial, a confidence booster that I appreciated even more after having been on my own for the preliminary hearing, before my grandparents knew about the abuse, and juvenile court, when they weren't allowed to come in. Later on, Debbie was there in court with us, too, going way beyond the expectations of the typical counselor-patient relationship. I had long felt like she'd become a trusted friend; it was heartening to see that reflected in her choosing to fly from New York to Tennessee, on her own dime, taking time from her busy schedule to sit through that insanity in solidarity with my grandparents and me.

Their support was critical—but that's all I had in my corner: five people, two of whom were paid to be there. The rest of the courtroom consisted of a mindless herd flocking in behind my mother, the cult of friends she and Mitch had quickly acquired in this time of need from the large Southern Baptist community in the area. It's striking to note that Grandma Sally, Grandpa John, and the rest of Mitch's family never attended a single court date. Still—and maybe spurred even more by his family's absence—Mom gathered up quite an elaborate cohort, filling row after row of benches on the side of the room behind the defense attorney's desk. The benches looked like church pews, and their group was a congregation amassed for prayer and preaching, awaiting deliverance. These people hardly knew my family, and most didn't know me at all, but were hypnotized by the version of the story Mom and Mitch liked to tell, in which they were innocent, godly folk whose names were being dragged through the mud by a bitter daughter. I felt like I was Alice in Wonderland, in a mockery of a courtroom, surrounded by characters so exaggerated they may as well have been cartoons.

Throughout the trial, the defense attorney, Craig, didn't hesitate to make me endure more victim shaming. He's the son of one of my mom's friends (hello, bias), and he had no experience with a criminal jury trial—which highlights the value that Mom, Mitch, and crew must have seen in the family-friend connection. You wouldn't suspect his limited experience based on his demeanor in the courtroom, though; he was always so cocky, as if he was better than everyone else there. He was a bully in an expensive suit. I repeatedly had to ask him not to use wording like "you had intercourse with your dad." "*He* had intercourse with *me*," I corrected him. I take no ownership of those actions and resented his implications that I did. He said in his closing argument that "If it was true, somebody would have seen, heard, known, what have you." Sorry to have to explain this to a lawyer, but that's rarely how rape works.

Craig pointed out with relish that I was a cheerleader, that I'd had several boyfriends. Between how young and naïve I still was during the trial and how overwhelmed I was by the entire process, the gravity of those offensive statements largely went over my head at the time—which, in hindsight, I'm not sure whether I'm relieved about or all the angrier. How dare he make such implications about a teenager? That my cheerleading uniform or my social life translated to sexual promiscuity? Only when talking to my grandparents after the fact did I realize just how inappropriate those comments were. What you're wearing or what you're doing doesn't mean you're asking for it! This is a lesson I've sometimes had to remind myself of, and one that I now try to pass on to other people. It's one of many ways I hope my story helps others in their own battles—or, better yet, helps them avoid the fight altogether.

Since my move to New York, without me around to contradict her version of the story, Mom had really been able to move in for the kill. Kristin was just one of many examples of how she got my friends into her clutches and twisted their perceptions. Several of them were working with Mom at the time; she'd gotten them jobs alongside her in an after-school program. So maybe they felt an allegiance to her, a debt owed.

The depths of that deception only fully became clear to me there in the courtroom. The twin sisters who had been my best friends since sixth grade—just after I'd moved to Tennessee, and just as Mitch was starting to groom me into a confused, timid girl—testified against me. When we first met, they had also moved there recently from another state. We had been strangers together in a new place; they had helped tether me at a time when I had felt so insecure.

Now, at this next great challenge of my life, the likes of which I'd certainly never known, like so many others they had shifted to the position of enemy, without warning. Last I'd seen them, even after I'd talked with them about what Mitch had done, we had been hanging out like everything was fine. I thought they had believed me. Now, I felt like if I approached them, a force field would repel me. It was a constructed divide, made by my mother's hands.

In an odd courtroom tradition, I guess to help document everything neatly for the record, Craig had the first of the sisters on the stand confirm my identity—and thus made us acknowledge each other's presence, that this was happening, that we were both participating, and not in friendly coop-eration.

"Is this Jessica right here?" he asked.

"Yes, sir," she answered.

I forced myself to look up and meet her eyes. *Yes, it's me,* I thought, my gaze burning toward hers. *I'm right here.* I felt so simultaneously on display and yet unseen.

Craig asked both of them about my reputation and my character for truthfulness.

"She was dishonest at times. She would tell lies, and...it would happen quite often," said the first sister to testify.

"She was not truthful. She was not an honest person," said the second.

There were no examples given or details sought. In fact, Craig was careful to instruct them not to share specific instances; so much of courtroom testimony is a careful dance around accusations of hearsay. Their purpose in being there, as witnesses for the defense, was to damn me and my credibility in those few brief sentences.

Hearing them speak, I felt unhinged. They had been friends whose secrets I had kept and whom I had trusted with my own, to whom I had laid bare so many pieces of myself, and at a time when it was increasingly hard to do so. We had had frequent sleepovers, whispering and laughing late into the night. We went to church and youth group together for years, spent countless hours hanging out at the mall, texted each other constantly. Our families had spent several Thanksgivings together. My moving away had loosened our ties a bit, as might be inevitable with a change of that magnitude, but they knew my truth before I left, knew about the chaos propelling the move. It made my chest ache to leave them, and our continued communication had helped keep me grounded and calm. It was agonizing to discover now, as they were speaking out against me publicly, that that trust, that entire foundation, had been irreparably broken. Was there no one who was themselves anymore, no one whose face and mannerisms I could still recognize as real? Had they all become these characters I was stuck with in an unending dream?

I wished I could stand up and scream and defend myself,

to call the twins out on *their* dishonesty. Thankfully, Laural was able to do so for me.

"You have told a few lies yourself, haven't you?" she asked the first sister, when it was time for her cross examination.

"Of course. I'm only human."

"You lied about boyfriends?"

"To my dad, yes."

"Lied about where you were going with people?"

"Yes."

"So, would you say everybody in the sixth grade probably told a lie?"

"Yes, I guess."

Laural then led the second sister through a similar line of questioning:

"You would say you were going one place and go somewhere else, do you recall that?"

"I have before."

"Would you say...every teenager at some point tells a lie?"

"Yes."

"So, are you a liar?"

"No. Maybe, yes. If I lie, yes, I'm a liar."

"So, then what you say doesn't really count either, does it, because we don't know if you're being truthful now or not?"

"I don't lie often. I have lied before. I don't lie often."

Of course, kids and teenagers tell lies. I have told lies—stupid, immature, trivial lies. I did not lie about what Mitch did to me. I would not lie about this, about something of this magnitude that takes over an entire life—multiple people's lives.

Laural had to take that time to counter what the twins and others said on the stand, because their sole reason for being there was to make me seem untrustworthy. As Laural would later point out in her closing argument, it seemed throughout much of the proceedings like *I* was the one on trial. I was not the one there, formally, to be deemed innocent or guilty at the mercy of the jury. I was required to be there by subpoena, just like any other witness. And yet I was continually being forced to defend the things I'd said and done—and justify what I *hadn't* said and done—and clear my name. I hadn't been accused of anything—other than by the defense.

"Most of the derogatory comments and the harshness has been directed towards her," Laural said. "And what did she do wrong? This is not a case where she's going to be found guilty of anything. But she has been the one attacked."

Unfortunately, the lack of physical evidence meant that the jury largely had to rely on weighing what my team and I said against what Mitch and his team said. Much of it came down to my word against his. In the US justice system, it's not up to the defense team to prove the defendant's innocence; rather, it's the prosecution's job to prove the defendant's guilt. In our case, that seemed to mean just as much, if not more so, that we had to prove my innocence and integrity. The defendant is not even required to testify (although Mitch chose to do so), nor is the defense team required to present any evidence (although Craig tried to do so). Like anyone on trial in this country, Mitch was given the presumption of innocence, but it often feels like victims like me aren't granted that same mercy.

The defense team's witnesses—called to the stand for the purpose of testifying in support of Mitch and, therefore, against me—also included my high school dance team coach and my pediatrician. In both instances, Laural was largely able to steer their testimonies in our favor.

As with the twins, Craig had brought in my dance coach

to characterize me as dishonest. But, after my coach shared a bit about the struggles she herself had had as a student, Laural asked her, "So, would you say that because you told lies and didn't hand in papers that you're not an honest person?"

"I don't think that you can draw those conclusions," my coach answered. "It doesn't necessarily mean that."

And Laural pointed out that Mom had taken me to see my pediatrician several months after the allegations had come out—after my two gynecological exams, including Sara's report that I had been sexually active for quite some time—yet didn't mention any of that to my doctor and, in fact, told her I was a virgin. My doctor told Laural on the stand that, yes, she would have liked to have known about those other visits and to have gotten their records, that she would have had concerns about my health if she'd known about the allegations against Mitch.

I hadn't told the doctor that I wasn't a virgin, either, but I thought maybe I *could* still consider myself a virgin on some level—like how some people look for technicalities as to how far they've gone, what they have and haven't done. These were actions done to me, ones I was hardly present for mentally, not ones I participated in willingly. To me, that was not sex.

Also testifying for the defense: my mother and Caleb, who continued into his teen years to be heavily influenced by our parents and, as far as I know, still is today. Until he removes himself from that atmosphere, if he ever will, he will not be able to form his own opinions. There is only so much I can stand to revisit of what they said in court, things I will never forget even if I let myself try.

Mom admitted to Laural that she'd gone through my texts

and phone records and had given that information to the defense attorneys.

"So, pretty much from day one, you were looking for evidence against your daughter, right?" Laural asked her.

"No," Mom said. "I was looking to find the truth."

But whatever she found, she did not give it to *my* attorney. She did not assist Laural in the investigation whatsoever. She only wanted alleged truths that might serve Mitch's case, not mine.

Laural also asked Mom about what happened after my second gynecological exam, the one she sought out with Sara, separately from the formal investigation.

"When that exam was done, and it didn't turn out the way you wanted it to, you didn't tell anybody, did you?" Laural asked.

"I told my friends," said Mom.

She did not tell the attorneys. Or the police. Or DCS. Because Sara's saying her exam showed a long period of sexual activity did not point toward Mitch's innocence.

When asked by Craig, Mom did say she loved me, which was some small, strange comfort.

Caleb did not.

Laural was the one to ask him.

"No, ma'am," he answered.

"But you guys were close until October of 2009?"

"Do I love her now or did I love her?"

"Do you now was the question."

"Do I now, no, I don't."

Fed up by the recurring sight of the skewed courtroom crowd, Tommy put out a call to his fellow police officers, asking anyone available to come in and sit with him behind Laural's desk, behind me, in a show of solidarity. The first time, about a dozen of them showed up together. It made for a pretty dramatic entrance, all of these uniformed officers filing in, making a point of patting both Tommy and me on the shoulder. Tommy told me that there's a universal understanding among that community that everybody wants justice when a child has been abused. I felt that in the way they showed up for me there. And they kept coming back. For the next several days in court, the officers would take a break from their desk work at the precinct, or would come in before or after the cases they were working were called up, or would sit with us while waiting for a call— they would give their time and attention to be there with me.

And then another kind of advocate showed up. Laural called Sara as a witness, so the jury could hear firsthand about what her exam had shown, rather than only listening to Mom and Laural debate it. Sara flew in just for a few hours to be there. She told the courtroom about her findings. "Her vagina expanded without any difficulty," she said. "It appeared to [be] a mature, sexually active vagina." She told them that what she saw indicated there had been long-term sexual activity. That tampons would not account for the extent to which my hymen was stretched. That dancing, cheerleading, the rape kit testing, and the other gynecological exam I'd had before hers would not have loosened my vaginal muscles. And that my mother didn't say much to her after Sara told her what she'd found.

After she stepped down from the witness stand, Sara walked directly in front of the jury box and over to me, bent down, and put her arm around me. In that moment, for once, it felt good to know how many eyes were on me. Let them see. Let them see me be held, heard, believed.

Just as I'd had to face my former friend when she identified me from the witness stand, I had to identify Mitch for the record. As if it weren't enough, weren't already too much, to feel his dissecting eyes studying me, to continually shift my weight in that pressure cooker of a room, I had to acknowledge that presence aloud, had to speak his name countless times, had to force my eyes toward his vicinity enough to say, "He's right over there," after Laural asked, "Who was the person who sexually penetrated you on all these different occasions? ... And is he in the courtroom? ... Where is he?"

Being on the witness stand is like being under a microscope, every facet of you examined meticulously, analyzed, scrutinized. It's like being naked in front of that room of enemies and strangers, everything you're used to keeping covered up now out in the open. It's a terrible necessity for a rape survivor in her quest for justice, to have the very subject of the crime on display when it begs to be hidden. The fact that I'd been through this a couple times already in the earlier hearings didn't make it easier. The short wooden wall in front of the witness stand provided some bit of potential cover. I wondered how much the jury, or Mitch and his attorneys, or my mother and her friends out in the pews, could see if I fidgeted my fingers in my lap, or crossed and uncrossed my ankles. I thought they could probably only see me from about waist- or chest-level up, so I kept my back straight and shoulders poised as best I could. But my hands and feet couldn't help but express some jitters, especially when I was working so hard not to let myself cry. For the most part, I tried not to think about how the spectators might perceive me. There was plenty else racing through my mind, anyway.

On the stand, I said things that I could not tell you now

from my own memory. The memories themselves—not just the recollection of sharing them with the court—have left me, thanks to the powerful scrubbing of dissociation. But my words are forever documented by dutiful stenographers in official transcripts; they are matters of public record.

That ink on those bound pages, multiple volumes thick as encyclopedias, will tell you, for instance, that the first time I woke up to find Mitch on top of me, I felt a heaviness. "He felt very heavy," I said. I imagine now the heaviness of sleep, a fog that lingers after you wake up mid-dream, the kind that leaves you unsure whether you've actually emerged from the dream or are still in the thick of it. It was, of course, also the heaviness of an adult man on top of a sixth-grade child. It was the heaviness of confusion, disbelief, fear.

"I was very scared," I said. "I could see his face from the night-light." The night-light that was there because I was scared of the dark. The face that I had trusted and loved, now digging a deeper trench for that fear. Laural wondered, as she told the jury, if my fear of the dark was because of Mitch all along, a fear of *him*, that I just didn't understand yet.

I told Laural and the courtroom of onlookers about Mitch's arms pressing against the bed near my shoulders, his heavy breathing, the smell and stickiness of his sweat, and having felt "sharp pains in my lower stomach area." My uterus. My cervix. Parts of my body I did not then have names for.

"Did anything go inside of you?" Laural asked.

"I believe so," I said, "but at the time, I was not aware of what sex was, so I did not understand what was going on."

This came up over and over again in my testimonies, how unfamiliar I had been with the things that were done to me, with the entire realm of sex, how young and naïve I was and should have been allowed to remain.

"You understood what had happened to you at that time, correct?" Craig asked me at one point.

"I was confused," I answered. "I didn't exactly know what sex was, but I knew it was bad."

I knew it was bad. And yet it was something I was being made to participate in. Of course I had been confused, afraid, silent. I did not want to be doing something bad. And I had trusted Mitch to be a protector, a guide, a responsible authority figure.

I testified about how I knew people shouldn't touch you in those places but that, when Mitch did, I was scared and didn't know to make a noise to try to summon help. About how the gynecological exam I'd had at the hospital the night of the police report was "whatever you normally get when you're sexually active, I believe."

Through Mitch's actions and in their aftermath, I was continually having things done to me that I didn't understand.

I was eleven years old when the abuse first happened. It was reported and began to be investigated when I was fifteen. I was speaking about it in the courtroom at nineteen. I'm telling you about it now at twenty-four. Between each of those ages I lived many lifetimes, became a different person several times over—and, thankfully, in the process, I let go of many of the details of what had happened. I did my best to recount them for the trial, but, even then, I often could only say, "It was a long time ago."

Many of the questions were designed to try to hash out the particulars of what happened when, partially to inform the charges against Mitch. But so much of it, including Laural's questioning of me, was mind-numbingly repetitive and particular: how old I was when a certain act of abuse happened, or even on what date it had happened; whether it was daytime or nighttime, before lunch or after lunch; whether or not I'd had dance practice that day. There was so much working against me in trying to answer those questions —in addition to the time passed since those events and the trauma and the awkwardness of discussing such vulnerable details in front of a courtroom, there was the blur created by the routine of it all, the numbness that had settled in early on and left so much of that time period a gray haze, even as I was living it. It's hard to separate one date from another, to lay out the specifics on display to be examined. I believe this is true about many details of most people's lives. The judicial process leading up to that trial had taken nearly four years, allowing for further fading of the events that had set this all into motion and the earlier conversations we'd had about them.

But Craig wanted the jury to question my truthfulness because of the details that I couldn't remember or that changed across my testimonies. He grew increasingly animated in his frustration as he questioned me, being asked multiple times by the judge and by Laural—and by me!—to lower his voice or not to interrupt me; he was so eager to point out any inconsistencies in an attempt to use them against me. Portraying me as a liar was critical to the defense's arguments. The jury's determination of Mitch's guilt or innocence hinged largely upon my credibility.

Craig often asked me about things I had said in the preliminary and juvenile court hearings four years prior, about the testimony I'd given then on particulars like dates and sequences of events. He would put transcripts from those previous court dates in front of me for reference and say things like, "So, this was an untruthful statement; is that correct?"

"At the time, it was not untruthful," I answered. How

could I possibly convey the way our memories and our very understanding of reality—especially when defined by trauma —are altered by the passage of years, by our evolving understanding of ourselves and our surroundings? Hadn't Craig— hadn't everyone in that room—experienced the same with the fragments of their own pasts? Couldn't they imagine how much blurrier those fragments would become when the mind wants desperately *not* to hold onto them?

Again and again, I was grilled about those kinds of things.

Craig: "Do you remember being asked about this before?"

Me: "I remember being on the stand for three hours and being questioned. I don't remember what I said or what was asked."

He would ask if I remembered having said this thing or that thing in the earlier hearings, and I would say, "I don't remember, but I may have. Do you have something saying I said it?"

I needed the transcripts as evidence of my own past. That dissociative haze had largely obscured those conversations, and their subject matter, for my own protection. I remembered that we talked about my dad sexually abusing me. I did not have the need nor the capacity to remember much beyond that fact.

Craig would then hand me a page from the transcript and say, "Does that refresh your memory?"

"No," I'd answer. "But since it's on there, I must have said it."

As Laural pointed out on my behalf, the preliminary hearing had included nearly one hundred pages of testimony about dates and times—on my first-ever day in court. At fifteen. Alone. And then we'd gone through the whole thing again four months later in juvenile court.

In those earlier court dates, there were times I felt like I *had* to remember a certain date, even if I didn't actually have any recollection of it. That's a frustrating sort of disorientation, to try to force your brain to connect dots it can't and won't.

Laural asked me on the stand how I'd been feeling at the time of those prior testimonies.

"Scared and frustrated and tired," I said.

So, as Laural then said, is it really any surprise or cause for doubt if, while in that sort of state, I didn't remember the date of a junior-high dance? That doesn't mean I wasn't raped before that dance.

One thing I am sure of is that memories change as time goes on. And there was, of course, another prominent influence in play by the time we were speaking in that courtroom. The physical distance I'd gained by moving to New York two years earlier had also provided my mind with the space and quiet it needed to gain clarity. Through my counseling sessions with Debbie, I'd recently been able to call some details back and begin making sense of ones that I had long ago blocked out.

"I've had time to think," I told Craig. "The more I talk about it, the more I remember."

The topic of lubrication, for instance, came up in multiple courtroom questionings. In the earlier sessions, I'd testified that Mitch hadn't used any. I don't know whether, at the time, I thought I'd remembered that he *hadn't* or that I just didn't recall him doing so. It didn't matter to me, at eleven or at nineteen, whether or not he'd used lubrication. It still hurt. It still was something I didn't want to be experiencing and so had worked not to remember. But, just a few weeks before my testimony for the trial, Debbie had been guiding me through some memories my brain had detached itself from, and a snippet came back to me, like a photograph starting to emerge in a darkroom.

"That's actually not true," I told Craig, when he brought up the topic again there at the trial and said, in summarizing the previous questionings, that none had been used. "He used to spit on his hand," I said.

Craig referred back to what I'd said in the preliminary hearing. "But now that's changed?" he asked.

"Yes," I said, "because now I've remembered more details."

"Is it fair to say...the further we've gotten away from these incidents the more you've remembered?" Craig asked.

"It is," I said, "but I'm not making them up."

We went through multiple rounds of this, like a nauseating carousel.

"You knew you needed to tell the truth when you testified to this previously, correct?" he asked me at another point.

"Yes."

"And you know you need to tell the truth now?"

"Yes."

"And the stories aren't the same, are they?"

"That does not mean that I'm not telling the truth."

Later, in his closing argument, Craig would say to the jury about my sharpened memories, "Ladies and gentlemen, this is way too convenient, okay." (He peppered many of his sentences with "ladies and gentlemen," like a melodramatic actor pretending to be a lawyer on TV.) He said I changed my testimony after being shown contradictions from the previous transcripts and realizing that the jury was "not going to buy it."

This extreme mischaracterization of me was especially infuriating coming from someone who liked to preach on and on about the truth. In his opening statement, he'd said of what the jury was about to hear from our side and his, "These stories cannot both be true." He was right—there was my version of reality and theirs, and they didn't make sense side by side. But he wanted the jury to believe the lies and misrepresentations from Mitch, my mom, Caleb, and the defense's other witnesses instead of my testimony—and, somehow, to believe that this was all happening because I hadn't wanted to get in trouble for making out with a boy on a couch four years ago.

"There are some things that you lie about, and some things you don't," Laural told the courtroom. Why would I have made this all up and still be maintaining a fictitious story four years later? Why would I disrupt my entire life, my family's lives, my friends' lives, and waste so many days being scrutinized and humiliated in court? By the time of the trial, Aaron and I had become little more than casual Facebook friends, checking in by text maybe every few months. Why would he show up to testify and lie for me? Why keep up the act, if it were only an act? Why would Tommy and Wayne—professional detectives with decades of experience, hundreds of these kinds of cases, under their belts—have lied for me? What did any of us have to gain from this? We were exhausted. We kept showing up and fighting because we knew we had to, to fight for the truth, not because we were clinging onto some ridiculous lie.

But that was the story the defense stuck to.

"So, you think all of this is about you catching her on the couch?" Laural asked Mitch while he was on the stand.

"Yes, ma'am," he answered. "I think it stemmed from that, yes, ma'am."

"And that's the only thing?"

"Yes, ma'am. That is the only thing."

Much of the rest of Mitch's testimony was a continuation

of his awkward dance around denying the allegations. When recounting his conversation with Wayne at our apartment after the report was first called in, Mitch told the courtroom that he'd said to Wayne, "I don't know anyone who would hate me enough to make that kind of phone call." He went on to describe his reactions as, "I didn't know what to make of it"; "I was just dumbfounded, you know"; and "I was like, whoa, you know."

When asked outright by Craig's co-counsel if he had ever had sexual relations or inappropriate contact with me, Mitch did, finally, say no. He uttered that syllable he couldn't seem to find during repeated questionings over the previous four years. He maintained it throughout a short series of questions: "Have you ever had any inappropriate contact with your daughter? ...Have you ever had sexual relations with your daughter? ...Have you ever touched her breasts outside of her clothes or inside of her clothes? ...Have you ever performed oral sex on her? ...These allegations that she's made against you, have you done any of this?" *No, no, no, no, no.* But anyone who wants to nitpick details I gave about times or dates or dance practice should find it hard to ignore the overarching inconsistencies when comparing Mitch's testimony to mine. His little refrain, in an exchange that lasted maybe one minute, was presented in contrast to my hours of laid-bare details of *penis* and *vagina* and *anal* and *period* and *tampon* and *hymen*. Upon the long-awaited emergence of that one syllable, *no*, a thousand continued intrusions into my body and mind and privacy were all supposed to be forgotten, dismissed, on the presumption that I would want to make up lies about these mortifying things, and that he was a good guy, and that guys perceived as good in their church or work communities couldn't possibly do bad things behind closed doors. As Laural told the jury, in order for them to believe the story that Mitch and the defense team presented to them, they would have to believe not only that Aaron and I were lying but that Tommy and Wayne were, too.

Much of what Craig said misrepresented and tarnished my character. One of the worst instances was when, in his closing argument, he came back to that update I'd given about Mitch having spit on his hand. "Ladies and gentlemen," he said to the jury, "I would submit to you that when she was fifteen this never happened, so she didn't know that having anal sex probably needed lubrication. And now at nineteen, now she knows how sex works, right."

Thank goodness for Laural, who used her own closing argument to put him in his place, calling that statement "a total humiliating, embarrassing, horrible thing to say to a young lady who has disclosed she has been raped by her father. There's no evidence of any other sexual activity that this child has had."

Craig didn't want to grant me leniency about any specifics, even though it was common throughout many people's testimonies not to be able to remember them. Just as my mom testified that she didn't know what time it was when I used to come into their room at night, or when her plane landed coming back from Africa, or when we were interviewed at the police station; just as Caleb got confused when questioned about the changed location of my bedroom because the two rooms looked similar, and he couldn't remember whether he'd slept in my room or his own on the first, second, or third night of that fall break; just as Mitch frequently mixed up details of the two different nights during fall break that Aaron had come over to watch movies, or confused the timelines of those evenings, or left out details until asked again, or said he couldn't remember...some of those kinds of particulars were lost for me, too. But because I couldn't remember if something happened at 8 p.m. or 9 p.m., I must be a liar and must have made the whole thing up.

I may not have had timestamps for everything, but I had held onto a lot of the little things. How Mitch smelled when he was assaulting me, that nauseating mixture of sweat and something burning. The swirls in the mirror. The glow of the light from the living room TV when Grandpa John would leave it on late at night, the glow of my night-light, the glow of the bathroom light under the crack in the door after Mitch would close himself in there. Why would my brain have stored details like those unless they had significance for some larger reason?

Craig confused details himself, which Laural seemed to take some delight in pointing out. As she was leading me, *again*, through the timeline of what unfolded once the police were called (hadn't this all been examined forward and backward and upside down? I didn't know how much more we could shake out of it), we discussed the rape kit exam I'd had at the hospital early the next morning, and she added, "So the Defense was wrong when they said you were there the same day; is that correct? ... So maybe he had his dates confused?"

I couldn't help but smile a little. Yes, he'd had his dates confused—just as I had, just as we all had, at points throughout this seemingly unending loop of a trial. I understood perfectly well how the details could all run together in an impenetrable blur, how one date could be confused for another before it or after it or even nowhere near it. But Craig wouldn't grant me that same understanding. I was the one who had been up all night to endure those procedures we were trying to recount now, not him. I was the one being asked to revisit trauma for the sake of analysis. I was the one who was raped.

At times, when convenient for his side of things, Craig did acknowledge that some details such as "silly dates" could fade over the years. But he did not think the first instance of assault could be one of them. In fact, in first selecting the jurors, he had been sure to assert—and made sure they agreed—that the first time a person has sex is "a pretty big deal," an experience they remember. I envy the people for whom that's true because of the positive emotions involved: love, lust, anticipation, a giddy rush of hormones, eager nerves, and anxious butterflies. I even envy the people who have what I assume are pretty common regrets about their first time, thinking maybe they'd rushed into it or wishing it had been with someone else they'd met later and cared about more. Because my "first time," and the many times thereafter, were chosen for me, forced upon me, the only emotions stirred up—the things that *have* stayed with me—are confusion, hurt, and anger.

Beyond my dissociating, the consistency of my testimonies was also complicated by yet another awkward technicality of the trial process that I was learning about the hard way: I wasn't allowed to talk about some instances—many instances, in fact—of abuse that had happened. In preparing for the trial, Laural and I had to put together what's known as a Bill of Particulars, laying out the specifics of each charge against Mitch. In our preparations, we had discussed—and the defense team and the judge knew about—roughly fifty or sixty incidents. I'm confident many more than that actually happened. But the Bill of Particulars covered ten, which meant we could only talk about those ten. This made some of the semantics challenging.

For the purposes of the charges and the discussions in court, the "first time" anything happened was in my bed in the middle of the night, waking up to Mitch on top of me. It was the first incident listed in the Bill of Particulars, forming the first charge against him, but it was not the first time he'd assaulted me. It was simply an early, specific incident that I could remember when making that list. When Tommy and Wayne had first interviewed me, the night of Mitch's initial arrest, I'd told them the "first time" was on the floor of my parents' bedroom, while my mom was asleep in their bed. I'm not sure now, and wouldn't have been sure then, either at fifteen or nineteen, which of those came first, just as I wouldn't have been able to list off all of the various acts that happened in between or after them. I just know that none of it should have happened and yet it happened many times.

The Bill of Particulars was requested by Craig's office, as it helps determine (and limit) what specifically the defendant is accused of. It associates a set of facts with each charge, and, once that's set, everything else is supposed to be off limits. We had first started putting it together the summer after the preliminary and juvenile court hearings, several years before we were gathered again to hash it all out there in big-boy court.

Because Laural recognized just how much all of the occurrences would blur together in my memory, if not be lost entirely, she had me focus on ones we could form the most proof around: did it happen leading into some other event that could help us place it in time? As Laural put it, "If fifty things happened in your bedroom, tell me about one of those that differentiates it from the other forty-nine." So, each incident listed represented countless others like it—but I was not supposed to talk about, nor were the attorneys supposed to ask me about, events occurring outside of the following:

1. I woke up in my bed to Mitch on top of me, penetrating me vaginally. I was eleven years old.

2. I wanted to go to the homecoming dance with my boyfriend. Mitch raped me in his bedroom. I was twelve.

3. I wanted to go to the school's Valentine's Day dance. Mitch raped me in his bedroom. I was around thirteen. I did not get to go to the dance.

4. I wanted to start a Myspace account. Mitch raped me in his bedroom. It was summertime, between eighth and ninth grade, not long after my fourteenth birthday, in June.

5. I wanted to hang out with my boyfriend before he went out of state for the summer. This was the first instance of anal sex, because I had my period. I was fourteen.

6. Later that summer, I wanted to get back together with that boyfriend, whom my mom didn't like. Mitch raped me in his bedroom. I was still fourteen.

7. These last few were all during the week Mom was away on her mission trip, while we were on fall break from school. I wanted to have Aaron over to watch movies. Mitch raped me. I was fifteen.

8. I wanted to meet up with Aaron at the mall. Mitch raped me anally, after which I felt a warm liquid back there.

9. This one had two parts to it. Mitch lifted up my shirt and kissed my breasts. Later that same day, I asked if I could go hang out with Aaron, and Mitch performed oral sex on me.

10. I again wanted permission to hang out with Aaron. Mitch raped me, and I texted Aaron about it having happened again.

Some of those events had multiple charges associated with them (for instance, both rape and incest); altogether, they added up to seventeen charges.

Even with attempting to limit testimony to that list, I think it's easy to see how one incident could get confused with another or the order could get jumbled, especially given the trauma. As Laural argued, "Is that really what you think somebody is thinking about when they're being raped? *Oh, I need to write down this time. I need to take this evidence.* She didn't even want people to know. She got through it because it kept her family together."

There were many other pieces of my own past that only became clear to me there in the courtroom. During his questioning, for instance, Mitch talked about his work in a factory that melted down plastic pellets to make car parts. He said the smell would cling to him, so he'd always shower and change his clothes when he first got home. "My wife doesn't like me smelling like oil," he said.

Only then did it finally become clear to me why I had always thought Mitch smelled like burnt popcorn. It was a harsh scent that would catch in the back of my throat, adding to how difficult it was to breathe when I was near him. I sometimes thought my brain was inventing this added layer of discomfort, my anxiety conjuring up all sorts of negative associations. But the smell was thick and inescapable; it would linger long after he'd been at the house to visit. It would hit my nose as I walked through the hallway, making it feel like we hadn't avoided each other at all, like he was right there, waiting around the corner.

I had recently quit a part-time job at Burger King because

the smell of the fryers made me so nauseous that I couldn't stand it. I hadn't even connected that consciously to Mitch's scent until that day in court. It's one of so many examples when the effects he had on me, the things he interfered with, continue to sneak up on me, even years later. To this day, if someone were to burn popcorn, I would need to get out. Thanks to living with Nana and Poppy, I could afford to leave the job, having very few expenses of my own. I recognize that now as a tremendous blessing—but it had felt good to work, to put my energy into something else, to build up a bit of savings and let myself believe I was starting to build something of a future, something of my own.

I had recently quit college too. The number of days I had to miss in order to be in Tennessee—not to mention the emotional toll of the whole process—made it impossible to keep up. I was afraid to disappoint anyone but knew I needed to give myself that break, in order to better focus on the challenge in front of me.

My mother was a natural fit in the circus ring of the courtroom. Her affecting the role of a self-absorbed teenager, surrounding herself with placating friends and carefree laughter, wasn't all that surprising, when I'm willing to look at it honestly. I assume some of it *was* an act, much like would be the case with a true teenager: pretending to be unfazed by what's unfolding, too cool to show weakness. There was an exaggeration to it, like an extravagant sports car with a blaring stereo—an overcompensation. But that behavior wasn't much out of character.

Knowing that my mom has image issues is the one thing that helps me to comprehend why she dug her heels in to stay on Mitch's side. Once she had decided and said out loud that she believed him and not me, there could be no turning back, or else she'd make herself look foolish for having chosen wrong before. For her to admit at any later point that the abuse *had* happened would mean she either had been oblivious to it or had turned her back to it and let it go on, either of which would ruin her image. Since I think she *did* know, I sensed a powerful shot of jealousy added to that stubbornness: she no longer saw me as a daughter but as the girl Mitch cheated on her with. I was the side chick, and Mom couldn't see past that to acknowledge that I wasn't in that role by choice. The verbal lashings she let me endure publicly, often at her own hand, branding me as dishonest and promiscuous, were her means of covering up what was really going on in her head, quieting those nagging thoughts. This couldn't possibly have happened at the hands of her husband, with her daughter, in her home, under her watch. Any one of those factors would mark her as flawed, let alone the combination of them. So she had to maintain that façade. She continued to pretend that everything was fine, other than the hassle I was causing.

Nana thinks that Mitch had manipulated Mom for many years, too, as part of his elaborate scheme of abuse. He had groomed her to be the strict parent, putting it into her head that I couldn't be trusted around boys and needed to be watched carefully. Then he would confuse us both by being the one to come to my defense and give me what I wanted, in contrast to Mom's punishments. It was all a dizzying game, which he played so expertly that we either weren't aware of the moves he was making or, later, couldn't avoid them even if we saw them coming.

That could be true. But while I recognize the role that all of these factors may have played for my mom, that doesn't mean that I accept or forgive the situation. She had enough chances, enough red flags, enough years, to have acknowledged the horrible truth and tried to help me—at the very least once it had all been presented to her on a carefully laid-out platter by not only her daughter but the detectives and doctors and DA. The one thing worse than being a rapist is standing behind one.

I think my mom is the reason the trial happened in the first place, the reason everything escalated with so much tension and dragged on for so many years. Mitch could have taken a plea deal early on in the process and avoided going to court at all. At the time, I would have greatly preferred that, just having it all done and over with, since I was so worn out from constantly having to relive the trauma and reiterate the same answers. But Mom was too aggressive to allow that approach. She would rather have the chance to throw a tantrum than let things play out quietly.

Even though my mother and I were not the ones on trial, it was terribly clear to everyone involved that she and I were on opposing sides. Laural and Tommy often escorted me out of the courtroom down a back stairwell to avoid crossing paths with Mom. Once, they tried to provide me a few minutes of sanctuary by leading me to a bathroom upstairs, in a quieter hallway where they knew no one else would be. But then we ran into Mom and Caleb sitting on the stairs. Mom pulled Caleb close to her, as if shielding him, and otherwise ignored my presence completely. She allowed me to step around them as if we'd never met before.

A Church Against a Child

THROUGHOUT THE TRIAL, IT SEEMED LIKE EVERYONE ON the defense's side was saying the same things, as if they were actors auditioning for the same part. Their lies matched the ones my mother had started like carefully coordinated decorations. It all seemed painstakingly rehearsed. A bunch of people submitted letters to the judge in support of Mitch, most of whom were their recently acquired friends from church and Bible study groups—friends who had only known my mom and Mitch after his arrest and had only heard one side of the story. Their letters talked about Mitch's strong faith and his great family-man outlook, like a checklist of requirements on a résumé that everyone pretends to meet. I couldn't help but wonder how specific my mom's instructions were in telling them what to write.

The words "integrity" and "character" were used in the vast majority of the forty-six letters. Many of the writers referred to "this injustice" they felt had been done to Mitch—even Caleb's friend, who would have been in his early teens at the time ("I humbly ask that you right this injustice," he wrote). Many of the openings and closings were set up in exactly the same way, and even those who otherwise weren't strong writers were miraculously formal in certain spots. It was like they were all given a template to fill in and a list of keywords to choose from. They said again and again that Mitch had grace, a gentle spirit, a great sense of humor; that he was a hard worker, was a man of God, and gave generously to charities. (The charity comment came up astonishingly often. How did so many of them know so much about his allegedly selfless generosity? Either he made a habit of bragging about it, or they were told outright to mention it.)

Their descriptions were so exaggerated that they made Mitch an unrealistically saintly character. *Nobody* is that good of a person, and certainly not him. Even if they insisted on believing he was a good man, that doesn't mean he couldn't have sinned. As Christians, we were taught that we were all sinners and should reach out to God for forgiveness. Lying about someone's sins or turning a blind eye to them certainly wouldn't make you pure in God's eyes! I felt like these people were only following the teachings that suited them, like they were clinging to the bits and pieces that served them well. What ever happened to "Love thy neighbor"? Or to bringing up children in the training and nurturing of the Lord? I have to wonder if any of these people actually read the Bible. I was a neighbor in need, a child looking for support and direction, and they chose instead to support a man who had done such awful things. As I sat in church, I felt like I was interpreting the readings and teachings in a different way than everyone around me. What *I* took out of the lessons didn't seem all that complicated to me: Don't judge people. Everybody makes mistakes. If you sin, ask for forgiveness. Try to be a good person.

There's a tone-deaf disconnect between the accolades

being thrown around so freely by these people and the actions they thought Mitch couldn't possibly have taken. While I don't agree with most of their descriptions, none of those traits would negate someone being abusive, anyway. A man can be funny and still be a criminal.

Since most of these people were lavishing praise on someone they'd only known during a narrow, carefully constructed window, allow me to set the record straight:

He was only a hard worker because he had to be. It was not in his nature. He was married to a shopping addict with a minimum wage job. They had filed for bankruptcy. The extra hours he took on were to help pay for his legal fees—an act of necessity after being accused of serious crimes, not merely something he felt compelled to do.

He was only active in the church after his arrest. Before that, it was like Mom was dragging him there. His devoutness became a front that Mom put up to make him seem innocent. She had been involved in the church for longer, but even her super-faithful phase really only came about after she returned from Africa—so, after Mitch's arrest. It probably seemed like the perfect cover: this faithful couple couldn't possibly be covering up something so horrific. Mom was always very good at putting on an act. She was well rehearsed. And clearly Mitch was a good actor too; he fooled all of these people into thinking he was a good guy.

He was a good father to my brother; that's true. But he was not a good father to me.

He was not generous. He was always very cheap. He didn't even want to give to the offering basket when it was passed around in church! Even as a kid, I knew there wasn't extra money to throw around. I don't know where the image of this endlessly charitable man came from—again, unless that's how people were told to perceive him.

As a kid, I did often think he was funny, but as I grew up and came to know the darkness he carried with him every day, I recognized increasingly how strange and sometimes manic his humor could be. At best, he was terribly immature; he would chase us and our cousins and friends around the house, letting us climb all over him—even once we were too big to be doing so. He encouraged frantic, disorienting chaos in his playfulness. He used to have some sort of a wrinkly wart or skin tag on his head. He would say it was his brain coming out, because he was so smart that there wasn't room. And then one day he just cut it off.

Like I said, manic. Chaotic.

Many of the letter writers spoke with a sense of authority, based on their age, long-time local residency, good relationship with Jesus, or the fact that they had known Mitch for a few years or had known people who had been abused. They seemed to think that these traits gave them some sort of expertise about the particulars of Mitch's case. I don't understand how they could so adamantly feel that they knew better than the detectives or the judge. Wayne hadn't wanted to believe the accusations, either, but he saw the truth in his first conversations with Mitch and with me. I wonder what these people would think of Mitch's character and heart if they watched his police interview!

At the same time, most of these people did not know me —had never met or spoken to me—and yet they felt entitled to critique my character and belittle my existence. Many of the letters, as well as comments on online articles about the trial, were just as lavish in their criticisms of me as they were in their glorifying of Mitch. They felt fit to cast judgment against me, to blame me for this heinous situation. Just like my mother and her Bible study friends who tried to cleanse me, they claimed to see the horror of the situation but were

186

looking the wrong way; they focused on me as an abomination without being willing to take an honest look at how I had been defiled. They pretended the things that had been done to me were things I'd done, ironically giving me autonomy where there was none, while stripping me of any sense of real power or voice.

I feel particularly disappointed by those who felt they were providing expert testimony because they knew victims of abuse. Why, based on *Mitch's* behavior, would they assume this case was different from the ones they'd known? Why not talk to me and see if the warning signs were the same, see if I reminded them of the broken shells of other victims? Mitch is proof of the fact that rapists aren't always easily identified, that they often know how to put up a good cover.

Some of the letters begged the judge to consider the altered lives of the family. What about *my* life? They spoke of "the family" as if I were not a part of it or not a factor to be considered, at least not compassionately. They prayed for my mom to be reunited with her husband, and Caleb with his father, while simply stepping around the ugly issue of the daughter. Despite claiming a deep love for our family, many either didn't mention me at all or referred to me coldly as "the accuser." Some of them wrote about Mitch's interactions with me having been only positive—people who, again, had never met me. How would they know? Clearly, they didn't.

In what still cuts through me with a stabbing irony, many of them talked about Mitch's compassion and his devotion to his family. They said they would trust Mitch with their lives and with their children's lives. I had trusted him with mine too.

For many, the lack of physical evidence made it too easy for them to disbelieve the charges. Just like Craig kept coming back to in the courtroom, they were willing to dismiss everything that I and those who testified on my behalf had said because there wasn't any definitively damning thing to point to: no semen, no fluids on the bedsheets or my clothes, no eyewitnesses. There was no evidence to find because Mitch controlled all of it. He covered his tracks expertly. Tommy testified that our apartment was "absolutely immaculate," "absolutely one of the cleanest houses I have ever been in." It would not have looked like a crime scene. Just because you can't see something firsthand doesn't mean it isn't true. And even if the detectives had torn the place apart, cutting out samples of carpet and hauling out the mattresses, of course they would have found Mitch's DNA, and mine, everywhere. As Tommy said in court, "the perpetrator and the victim lived in the same residence." There was not going to be any shocking discovery of hairs or fingerprints to reveal that the accused had in fact been at the scene of the crime. We both lived at the scene of the crime.

The twins wrote letters, too, about how much time we'd spent together growing up and about how, despite being young and therefore "confused" at the time of the abuse, they later came to understand what it would do to the family if Mitch were to be found guilty. Like so many others, but even more heartbreaking, they wrote about supporting the family, as if I weren't part of that consideration. What about supporting their friend?

It was also hurtful to read some people's comments about the loving relationship between Mitch and my mom. They highlighted the neglect I was feeling—that I still sometimes feel—and the shift Mom had made in aligning herself with Mitch and against me. One woman who had worked with Mitch wrote of him and Mom: "Although they were going through an obviously stressful time, you could see their love and support just being in the same room." No one ever would have said that about Mom and me. She may have claimed to be neutral, or even at times tried to portray herself as a doting caregiver, but there was no aura of love and support surrounding us. All anyone would see between us was distance, the coldness of strangers or even enemies. For others to comment on the noticeable bond between Mom and Mitch emphasizes how fake she was in saying that she was experiencing any doubts or difficult decisions as to whom she should believe. She had made her choice before we'd even left the police station. Maybe before she'd even gotten there. Maybe years before.

A letter from my uncle, Mitch's brother, expressed "confusion" over several things that left him unable to believe my story—things I could have answered, if only he had bothered to talk to me. I will answer them now.

He was confused as to how abuse could exist amidst the "normal" things he knew Mitch did with Caleb and me, like teaching me how to drive, going to Caleb's baseball games and my dance recitals, or taking us to Dairy Queen for ice cream—things that might have made us seem like an everyday, happy family.

Yes, those things did happen—and between those normal things, Mitch would rape me. The return to "normal" behavior was part of the routine, after each instance of abuse.

He was confused as to how someone working eighty-plus hours a week "would have had the time to do the things he's accused of."

It didn't take long. It only takes a second or two to touch someone. And the rape would usually last for just a couple minutes, though it's misleading to say "just" when even seconds of that kind of unwanted, nauseating activity feel like an unbearable eternity. It was always quick, because he was trying not to get caught.

He was confused about their father's presence in our home, just as Mom had been, as if that extra set of eyes and ears would have prevented any such activity.

It didn't matter who was around. Mitch routinely violated me while his wife was asleep right next to us.

An uncle from my mom's side of the family and his girlfriend both wrote letters that talked about their children's loving bond with "Uncle Mitch." That family had not been on good terms with Mitch, nor had much contact with him, for about eight years at that time.

So many lies, so much blatant ignorance of the truth. I still don't understand how these people could so blindly defend Mitch and ignore the pleas of a hurting child. I guess he and Mom were very convincing in their acting.

They convinced their followers that *I* was the one putting on an act. What would I have to gain from this? Why would I want *that* kind of attention, or to put myself through such stress and embarrassment for the sake of some strange sort of revenge? Their argument that I was mad because Mitch caught Aaron and me fooling around falls apart quickly when you take just a minute to think it through. If I were that embarrassed about kissing on the couch, why would I then elect to get my revenge by telling detectives, doctors, CAC and DCS officers, a judge, a jury, and a courtroom full of strangers such intimate details about my body and my sexual experiences? I endured all of that only because I knew it was what I *had* to do to have any hope of justice.

Since moving to Tennessee, we'd gone to church every week as a family—every week, that is, until I filed the report against Mitch. My mom ripped me from that atmosphere like a weed. Removing a child from church who allegedly needs salvation might seem like an odd choice of punishment, but, in doing so, she was removing me from my friends (though I didn't know how effectively she would sever that tie until they showed up on the witness stand) and from yet another layer of familiarity and comfort.

After a couple months, she started taking me there with her again on occasion, but she wouldn't let me go to the youth Bible study class beforehand, where my friends and Aaron were. She kept me right next to her, like she couldn't trust me if I wasn't under her close supervision. It was no longer a space of refuge for me; Mom had told everyone our business, and once again it felt like they were all staring at me. Often, they really were—Mom had told Nana that there were a lot of eyes on me at church, watching the "bad things" I would do: talking to Aaron, holding his hand, "even" kissing him a couple times. We weren't being inappropriate; he was the closest friend I had at that time and such a crucial source of support. Being with him made me feel safe. But Mom and her accomplices didn't want that for me. They wanted me to feel guilty, to be reminded constantly of what (as they saw it) I had done to Mitch—as if I weren't already playing all of that messy agony on a continuous loop in my head. As if I hadn't already suffered enough from the abuse itself. They were doing all they could to leave me unmoored.

In fact, my first day back at church after that forced hiatus is a vivid memory, another one of those surreal moments when I felt like—and wished—I was dreaming. It was a jolting turn of events when Mom woke me up that Sunday morning to say I needed to go to church. Shortly after we got there, before the service started, Mom's friend Ruth grabbed my arm and pulled me up toward the altar. I tried to pull my arm away, but her grip only tightened, her bony fingers cold against my skin, leaving me no choice but to stumble awkwardly behind her up the aisle. Mom just sat there and made no attempt to help me.

At the altar, Ruth leaned in, close enough that her red curls brushed my shoulder, and whispered, "Your dad loves you and prays for you every night."

I felt sick—nauseous, dizzy. I hated anyone whispering close to me after how many times Mitch had done so, and the warm tickle of her breath was invasive and irritating, like a mosquito buzzing. And those words she threw at me—which, like so many from the church community, had the veneer of good intentions but in truth were only meant to shame and control me—only added to the churning in my stomach. I couldn't find any words in response, and my body felt awkward up there at the altar, in front of everyone as they filed into their pews. Kneeling there, with Ruth's hand still tight around my arm, I felt like a sacrifice.

When I got back to my seat next to Mom, I hurled a whisper of my own at her. "You know, I really didn't want to go up there."

"Well, I didn't *know* she was going to do that!" Mom replied.

I found that hard to believe, given how eagerly she had roused me out of bed to come with her that day, after not wanting me there for so long.

Despite the many reasons there may have been to question it or seek some distance from it, my faith remained strong throughout everything I went through. Perhaps it was because I always had my own vision of it anyway. I took the church's teachings to heart and applied them to my life and my actions as best I could, and when the actions of others in that community didn't seem very Christian to me, I just prayed that God would help to guide them back in the right direction. I prayed a lot for my mom and Caleb, too, and for us all to be led through this horrible test. I often needed to rely on that faith and am grateful to have had it and held onto it. Sometimes, the darkest storms only strengthen our belief in the light.

My faith is also what kept me from ever seriously contemplating harming myself. Sure, there were sometimes flickers of those kinds of thoughts, given the depths of the darkness I was facing, but my faith gave me the strength to know that better days would come, even when that seemed like the hardest thing in the whole world to believe. I knew it was all ultimately out of my hands, that there was a greater power at work who would guide me through it all and make it okay in the end. I *had* to believe that.

Mitch had also been removed from the church, because the nature of the charges against him meant he wasn't allowed to be around children. So, he and Mom had started going together to a few Bible study groups instead, which is where they met many of the friends who proclaimed his innocence. But despite his formal exclusion, the church did not cast him out as they had done to me. In fact, the flock of his supporters from the congregation and their other religious circles helped fund his many attorneys throughout the years of proceedings—some of whom have reputations for charging six figures—as well as his rent and utilities, since he'd been displaced from home. They would have bake sales and such to raise money for him, a big, showy effort. The judge was a deacon in another Southern Baptist church in the area and admitted—only halfway through the trial, during a bench conference with the attorneys—that he knew Craig and his mother and much of the church group personally, that they had been guests in each other's homes. Laural said it made her feel sick, heartbroken, because if she asked for a mistrial because of the bias, I would have to testify all over again.

We'd be starting from scratch, except for the fact that the defense would have that many more pages of transcripts to pore over for discrepancies to torture me with. The judge granted the defense's requests to have some of our best evidence removed—evidence that undoubtedly would have helped convict Mitch on the higher-level charges and hand him a much harsher sentence, like those recorded interviews at the police station. He cried when he delivered Mitch's sentence.

Though I knew nothing of the legal system before being thrown into this fray, and was coming to know it through what felt like a blender filled with jagged rocks, I was pretty confident at the time that what was unfolding around me was unconventional. Now, with the benefit of clearer rearview vision, I still can't fathom how this sort of thing is able to happen, especially in our allegedly progressive time and country. It felt like something quite a ways beyond a defendant's right to presumed innocence, like a contamination of the process by the heavy hand of this outside influence. There was no separation of church and state here.

The church supporters' presence spilled out of the courthouse. One of them had a big house nearby, and on breaks and after each day's session, the flock would go there and pray. As Laural and I walked into and out of court each day, their group would be gathered on both sides of the walkway, heckling. And Mom was right in the thick of it all. She would give speeches from the courthouse steps, talking to her masses.

Holding fast in my own little niche of faith served me well during that strange time, and now I've found comfort in moving away from it a bit. I feel like I *had* to let go of it, at least of the parts that had been dictated to me and inscribed upon me. The teachings of that community in Tennessee had too often made me question myself and my truth. That kind of faith was tying me down. I feel freer now without it.

Still, I'm grateful that it helped carry me through that time, when it was tested unlike ever before or since. It taught me patience, perseverance, and hope. Most importantly, it taught me to believe in *me*.

No Child Deserves to Live in Fear

LAURAL SAID MITCH USED THE ADOPTION PAPERS LIKE A marriage license. She wondered if he was in love with me and therefore said he hadn't raped me because, maybe, "in his mind it was something else." I don't know if he thought I was his property, or thought he loved me in a way different than a father normally loves a daughter. I can't know what he was thinking. What I do know is that he stole years of my life from me, not only through the abuse but through the additional years I spent fighting it, and, as the trial neared its end, I was desperately ready to reclaim my life as my own.

In her closing arguments, Laural told the jury that what they'd heard over the past week wasn't a matter of two stories, mine and Mitch's, like Craig had said but of three—with Craig's being the third. He'd created his own version by choosing to focus so much on the particulars of the prior transcripts, nitpicking sixteen lines out of thousands, confronting me with a volume more than two hundred pages thick of my own words, which I'd never read, and creating a spectacle out of those innocent words.

Craig relied on that spectacle to shift the focus onto me, to put the victim on the defensive and take the attention off of his client. "He's a nice guy," Craig said to the jury about Mitch. "I mean, you guys heard him testify. He didn't have to testify. He got up here and told you the truth, ladies and gentlemen." By comparison, I guess, I was supposed to look like a liar and not a nice person.

This performance reminded Laural of the movie *The Wizard of Oz*. She asked the jury to think about how Craig had flailed about with this page and that page, as if saying, "Pay no attention to the man behind the curtain. Look at me, look at her. Pay no attention to this man...who initially could not say it didn't happen." My heart swelled as she spoke. It really did feel as if the curtain Mitch had long been hiding behind had come crashing down, and yet Craig wanted everyone to ignore the fact that Mitch was sitting there, pulling the strings, manipulating everyone. Craig wanted them to focus only on *him*, his show, his story, and thereby see me as the one worthy of suspicion.

Throughout all of their charades and shenanigans, I had stood my ground, stood by the facts of my past. "She's said the same thing since [four years ago], when she could have gone on with her life," Laural told the jury. "She didn't have to be here at all. She had no reason to lie, and she lost everything. Which of these two had the most reason to lie? Which of them got caught in a story that they couldn't get out of?"

I had sat there through seven days of criticism, embarrassment, baseless attacks on my character, and discussion about the size of my tampons. I had had plenty of opportunities to take my accusations back, to say these things hadn't happened. "At any time over four years, she could have made this go away," Laural said. But I never did, because it was the truth, and it needed, finally, to be heard.

The judge gave the jury many pages of detailed instructions about each charge against Mitch and what Laural needed to have proven in order for them to find him guilty of it. Once again, there were a lot of semantics involved, such as whether it was proven that Mitch had acted knowingly, intentionally, or recklessly. Each charge had "lesser included offenses" corresponding with it, meaning if they found him not guilty (or had a reasonable doubt about his guilt) of the initial charge, such as rape of a child, they would acquit him of that offense and then consider the next step down of sorts, which in that instance would be *attempted* rape of a child. If they found him not guilty (or had a reasonable doubt about his guilt) of all of the lesser included charges within a count after going through each, one by one, then they had to acquit him of that entire count. They could only find him guilty of one offense within each count. And each verdict had to be unanimous. Any lingering hesitation among any one of the twelve jurors meant Mitch could not be found guilty of that charge.

Laural is confident that the jury went over everything carefully and weighed the evidence. I don't remember how long they deliberated for. It felt like both an eternity and a flicker.

The judge read the verdicts out, count by count, my stomach doing somersaults throughout:

1. Guilty of the lesser included offense of simple assault.
2. Guilty of the lesser included offense of aggravated sexual battery.
3. Guilty of the lesser included offense of aggravated sexual battery.

4. Guilty of the lesser included offense of sexual battery.
5. Guilty of the lesser included offense of sexual battery.
6. Guilty of the lesser included offense of attempted incest.
7. Guilty of the lesser included offense of attempted incest.
8. Guilty of the lesser included offense of attempted incest.
9. Guilty of the lesser included offense of attempted incest.
10. Guilty of the lesser included offense of attempted incest.
11. Guilty of the offense of incest.
12. Not guilty.
13. Not guilty.
14. Guilty of the offense of statutory rape by an authority figure.
15. Not guilty.
16. Not guilty.
17. Guilty of the offense of sexual battery by an authority figure.

Altogether, that's twelve felonies and a misdemeanor. Aggravated sexual battery is a higher-level felony and required that Mitch be taken from the courtroom into police custody.

Nana and Poppy felt happy about the guilty verdicts, like justice had been served. For me, though, it was a sad day. It solidified everything that had happened between us and made it feel not only more real, but more permanent. As the judge was speaking, I picked a tile on the floor and stared at it the entire time. It was like an out-of-body experience, or maybe more dissociating—I was there physically, but not mentally, at least not completely. I couldn't be.

I remember Caleb begging to hug Mitch as they prepared to lead him away. The bailiff wouldn't allow it. I wished he would. I wanted Caleb to have that moment. Maybe it was just a wave of sentimentality at this turning point in our collective lives, and I'm sure it was influenced by the guilt I still carried about setting this all into motion, but my role as sister—and as daughter—never really went away, at least not in my mind.

As they put Mitch in handcuffs, Nana and Poppy tried to prevent me from looking. But I knew I needed to see it. Permeating through the sadness, there was a flicker of hope, of relief. Finally, tentatively, I felt a little safer.

Several of the jurors came up to me after it was all over, hugging me and saying they wished they could have done more, but too much evidence had been removed. It felt odd to know that they believed me, that they saw the same truth I had carried quietly for so many years. Laural pulled me aside in the parking lot and confided in me that she had also been abused as a child. She said, "My mother didn't believe me, either."

This feeling of camaraderie, of comfort and understanding, was still so foreign to me. I welcomed it but didn't quite know what to do with it. It sat awkwardly in my chest, a mixture of pride and embarrassment. Maybe I was exhausted from so much time in the spotlight. Or maybe I just wasn't used to having others step into that light and reassure me.

A swarm of church supporters came to Mitch's sentencing, a couple months later. When Laural and I first walked into the courtroom that day, there were still other cases being heard. We sat off to the side to wait our turn. When the judge called our case up, he asked the rest of the courtroom to clear. Everyone else left sitting there was in a large cluster on one side of the room, maybe fifty or even a hundred of them. Their shirts were all white, as a symbol of their solidarity and, I guess, of Mitch's alleged purity. I found out later that they called themselves White Shirts for Wilsons—the plural name applying only to Mitch, my mom, and Caleb, of course. I remained outside of their concept of the family unit that they were so intent on protecting. Much of this group, the flock of church and Bible study friends, had long been vocal in throwing their support behind that estranged family unit, but now there were even more of them, and now they had this symbol, amplifying their presence as if screaming at me even while they had to try to remain quiet in the courtroom. They even had a Facebook group—managed by my mother—to rally their troops and commiserate about how unfairly they felt Mitch was being treated.

As the crowd dissipated to reveal that sea of white, my heart fell down into my churning stomach. We were about to find out Mitch's fate—and, by association, mine and my family's—and, in that sudden face-slap of a moment, I was being reminded all too clearly just how stacked the deck seemed to be against me. Did all of these people really believe Mitch was innocent? Still? How could they see me there—a shy child, waiting anxiously for the justice I'd been needing for years—and feel nothing but misdirected anger and blame? And, even after everything I'd been put through, the thought that nagged loudest in my head was: were they right?

My pulse was in my throat as I read my victim impact

statement. I hadn't known what to write initially—I had already had to speak in front of the courtroom so many times, revealing so many more personal details than I ever could have imagined; what more could I pour out?—but Laural encouraged me to speak from the heart, to use this as an opportunity to summarize one more time the effects that Mitch's crimes had had on me.

Looking back at it now, I'm struck by the fact that, while I did of course talk a bit from my perspective as a victim, I was already looking to shift my focus to the future, to what I could become on the other side of all of this.

"My name is Jessica," I read. "I am nineteen years old. A lot of you in this room only know me by name but not as a person. I would give almost anything for the ones I love. I am a forgiving person. I don't sleep well at night because I'm afraid of the dark, afraid of what may be waiting for me when I turn off the lights. Some of you say I have evil inside of me— I say I have God inside me and a strength—a strength that I cannot describe. I have the ability to forgive others no matter what, just like I have done with my father. Everyone says the things he has done will forever haunt me. I say they will not define me. I love my brother and mother unconditionally. I pray every night for them. Everything I have said today and during the trial has been the truth. My father's fate can be determined by the judge. I will determine my fate."

Each charge, individually, carried a potential sentence of eight to twelve years in prison, and the judge could have made them consecutive (finishing one sentence only to begin the next), adding up to decades. Instead, he made the sentences concurrent. Mitch was sentenced to a total of eight years in prison, followed by seven years of supervised probation.

When the time came to go to court yet again six months later because Craig had appealed the guilty verdicts, Laural urged us to get more people there, to help the judge see a strong showing of support behind me. She and Nana and Poppy had seen how much the presence of the White Shirts had shaken me, and they were furious. It was time to even out the sides.

Laural connected us with a group called Bikers Against Child Abuse (BACA), an all-volunteer, worldwide organization that supports victims of sexual, physical, and emotional abuse. They call themselves "the keepers of the children," and I quickly came to see how seriously they commit to that mission. Nana, Poppy, and I arrived at the hotel where we'd be staying and were introduced to the group there. They had come in from as far as California and Washington, from all over the country, filling fifty of the hotel's rooms and spilling over into another. They stationed themselves outside our room in shifts, all day and night, my own personal bodyguards.

Everyone in the group goes by an alias, a "road name," and they encourage each of the children they work with to choose a name of their own. From BACA's perspective, it offers the victims added privacy and protection; beyond that, it helped me take a step out from the shadow of my shyness and feel welcomed into their circle. It felt quite literally like becoming a member of a tribe, after being an outcast for so long in my own community, my own home. It didn't take me long at all to decide on my road name: Justice. I felt so proud to carry that name. Justice was what I had been seeking for years; taking it on as a name made me feel in control of achieving it. Justice was no longer something I was hoping and waiting for but something I would command. That name reminded me that I was a voice not only for my own battle but for others' too. It reassured me that I was doing the right thing by continuing to fight.

Among the patches on the bikers' vests was their motto: *No Child Deserves to Live in Fear.* I was in awe of how powerfully this group spoke to all that I had been dealing with. As I stood among these two hundred tough-looking people I'd never met before, their swarm of dark leather towering over me, my shyness and self-doubt stepped out of my way. I felt bolstered up, rejuvenated. Positive energy surged around me, a humming reassurance that everything was going to be okay.

I appreciated how much effort the BACA members put into getting to know me as a *person*, not just a victim of abuse. I wasn't a statistic to them or a name on a list of contacts to make. They didn't want to know what had happened to me, but who I was and what mattered to me. That helped me to remember that there was much more to me than what had been dominating my time and energy for the last several years, that this was something I was at the height of dealing with, but it did not define me or what my whole life would be about.

When we were chatting one day, I mentioned that I loved to shop, and that little tidbit was all they needed to set into motion an amazing day for me, a day when I could just be myself—just be a kid—and let the weight of the abuse and the ongoing court drama fall away. Rarely the type for subtlety, they took me to the mall as a giddy (and probably completely out of place) member of a full-on motorcycle herd. I rode on the back of the chief's bike, and others rode behind and all around us. I felt like I was a celebrity with a security entourage surrounding me.

Nana went with us. As the bikers brought out dozens of outfits for me to try on, one handful of hangers after another, I kept looking over at Nana, eager but a little nervous, asking her, "Can I have this? Is it okay if I take this one, too?" She told me later that she couldn't help but say yes, because she was just so happy to see me happy—even though all the while she was doing some mental math and thinking, *Holy cow, this is gonna be 3-, 4-, 500 dollars...*

It turned out she had no need to add up those price tags. As she pulled out her credit card at the register, the cashier told her with a smile that the bill was already covered.

I was practically skipping as I walked out of the mall, surrounded by my newfound crew of guardians and friends, bags from my favorite stores dangling from my L-shaped arms, from elbows to wrists. I felt delightfully spoiled. For the first time in years, I felt beautiful.

The bikers also bought me earbuds and iTunes gift cards so I'd have music to listen to in court if I got overwhelmed. As if all of that weren't enough, they took up a cash collection for me and raised a few hundred dollars. They're a nonprofit group, and they gave so much to me. I will forever be grateful to them and forever be changed because of them.

Despite the number of children they help every year, BACA sees our bond as a forever one, too. They told me that I would be a part of their family for life. I take comfort in that even now, as a young adult, knowing I could turn to them any time I need reassurance and knowing that they continue to help other kids like me.

BACA's involvement with my case was an important turning point, a huge confidence booster. Now I not only had guilty verdicts corroborating my story but a badass group of bikers acting like my guard dogs. While I knew how kind-hearted they were—sweet and noble to the core—the outward vibe they gave off was intimidating, in the most wonderfully empowering way. This time, I walked through the square to the courthouse surrounded by my entourage, protecting me like a force field. This was the same square that had so recently, time after time, been cluttered with the name-calling, shame-hurling church group, led by my mother. This time, their group of twenty-some people was dwarfed and drowned out, and they kept their distance. Someone from BACA went with me everywhere, escorting me to the bathroom or to get food, waiting with me in the hallway. They helped me reframe my thinking to focus on the job I needed to do: get in, testify, and get out. They orchestrated the ushering in and out like a security team shielding a celebrity from the paparazzi. Their constant presence sent a clear message that I was not to be messed with. It felt amazing to overshadow the flock of white with this muscular, tattooed wall of dark leather.

Fewer White Shirts even bothered showing up after that first court date for the appeal. Their Facebook group disappeared. The online commentary bashing me stopped. I don't know if people no longer believed my mother so readily or if they simply lost steam, but either way, it was a welcome change of pace. I only wish we'd gotten BACA involved sooner. They were my guardian angels.

Mitch's appeal was denied. As were the next four.

Even though—or perhaps because—I had fought so much of the battle alone, sometimes I think I found my best self in that courtroom. Maybe it took being coerced into silence for so many years in order for me to finally use my voice. I had been thrown into an entirely new world, filled with legal jargon and postponed dates and seemingly endless, exhausting testimonies, and instead of letting that overwhelm me, instead of retreating into a quiet corner like I may have wanted to so many times, I allowed it to strengthen me and propel me forward. The swell of emotion and stress carried me along like a roaring wave. It was always looming and threatening to swallow me whole, but I refused to let it drag me under.

Debbie said she would have expected me—the version of me she'd known up to that point—to crumble during the trial. I can't blame her; I had been reduced to so little self-confidence, so little self-*worth*, that far less taxing things were enough to leave me trembling and incapacitated. How could I withstand months of courtroom drama? How could I face my mom and brother, who wouldn't even acknowledge me, and speak these awful truths in front of them and countless strangers, and maintain some semblance of sanity?

But Debbie said she knew I would be okay after she heard the voice I summoned on the witness stand. While my move to New York had been detrimental to me in many ways, neither my mother nor I had realized at the time that, in other ways, she had handed me a gift. The ugly weed she had planted by shipping me off there would eventually—after hefty investments of time, patience, and care—blossom into a beautiful flower that I never expected to see. I don't want to think that the additional trauma I endured in New York was necessary, but it inevitably became part of my foundation; it further toughened me, focused me, emboldened me. It freed me to become a new and better version of myself, allowing me to find my voice and start using it. In my sessions with Debbie, I'd gained courage and more confidence in myself and my worth than I'd ever felt before. And at home with Nana and Poppy, I was finally with people who believed me and supported me; I no longer had to hide my truth or my vulnerabilities. That was scary at first but ultimately helped complete the transformation I don't think I ever would have been able to make in Tennessee.

By the time Mitch, my mom, and the defense flock saw me again in the courtroom, I was not the same meek, shy little girl they last knew. I surprised even myself with that newfound confidence, but I clung to it like a life preserver in those tumultuous waters. As Craig badgered me with his spewed interrogation, speaking over me to jump to his next convoluted point before I'd even had the chance to complete a sentence, a voice decibels louder than I'd ever owned came from my mouth: "Can you wait until I answer the question?"

Debbie's squinting smile was like a high-five across the courtroom.

Banishing the Ghosts

I'VE KNOWN FOR YEARS THAT I WANTED TO WRITE THIS book. It's partially a way to continue to drive out the ghosts I mentioned before, the trauma that still ripples like after-shocks. It took me a while to be ready to tell my story, because I worried that people would question and judge me, as had been my experience throughout so much of this ordeal. I hope that sharing this now will help not only me but others too.

We tend to hear about abuse happening out at parties or colleges or remote locations; we don't hear about the things that are happening at home. We hear a lot about "stranger danger," but for me, my own home was the danger. These are the questions I want asked, the voices I want heard. These things need to be talked about.

Even though Mitch was convicted, I often wonder in frustration if he really lost anything. His prison sentence is taking eight years of his freedom—less than the time that passed between when he first abused me and when he was convicted. It's the minimum sentence. It's not nearly enough. And when he gets out, his wife and family will be waiting for him. He will resume his life, although that life will be minus a daughter.

Meanwhile, my sentence continues. I feel that all of this has only affected me more over time. I remain less trusting and more vigilant; it's like I've given my friends and the guys I've dated their own trial, their own sentence—we're all forced to wait it out as I see how things unfold. And I keep myself under close examination, too. I have to figure out how to control my feelings and how to express them in non-aggressive ways. Most times when I'm upset, I don't express it all; I let it bottle up until it explodes into a big fight later on. I certainly didn't gain a foundation in healthy communication from my childhood, and any confidence or self-awareness I did have was then banished by Mitch and by the trial.

I sometimes have to remind myself that I'm not lying. The defense tried so adamantly to brand me as the wrongdoer that it could shake even my own stance. Had I misremembered? Exaggerated? Confused myself? While my rational mind knew without question that I was the victim and Mitch was the criminal, the courtroom experience was its own kind of trauma and often left me timid in new ways. My mom testified that I had a tendency to do things just for attention. That wording crawled into some deep crevice of my brain and still refuses to leave, even today. Sometimes I worry that the people closest to me don't believe me. And sometimes I still feel guilty, like if I hadn't said anything, things would have been okay, and my family would still be together.

The extent to which Mitch and my mother warped my reality is perhaps most prominent when I admit that I was kind of hoping the court would find him not guilty. I had seen my mom and brother so broken down by the whole situation, and I was already working on setting up a new life for myself in New York. Despite what Mitch had done to me, I thought maybe the conviction was unnecessary. Despite the sentence being the minimum, I thought maybe it was too much.

Now, thankfully, I'm far enough on the other side of all that chaos that I can see how the guilty verdicts help to keep a criminal away from me and from other people. I hope that outcome sets some sort of example and sends a message that the things Mitch did to me were not okay—they were not expressions of love or protection; they were not innocent mistakes or lapses in judgment. They were crimes, they were inexcusable, and they destroyed a family. Mitch's actions did that, not mine.

If my story can help even one child who is being or has been abused, or one parent who has been questioning warning signs and unsure of how to help their child, then I'm happy to share it. It has taken a long time for me to feel empowered by this journey, and there are many days that I'm still shaky. I hope I can help others take their own first step— or second, or hundredth—toward healing, and toward hope. I felt so alone while I was enduring the abuse and throughout the aftermath. Sometimes I still feel alone with the memories of it and the remnants. So, perhaps the most important message I could leave you with is that you are not alone.

You are *not* alone.

You are not guilty.

You are not wrong or dirty or tainted or a bad person.

You are one piece of an enormous, vibrant world that continues to evolve and to offer beauty every day while waiting for you to emerge and discover it. I've come to feel proud of my piece in that puzzle, and deserving of it, and hopeful for what's coming next.

Those are emotions I wouldn't have thought possible just

a few years ago. But I found them, and I'm holding tight to them. You can find them too.

Just pull back the curtain.

Afterword
by coauthor Valerie Dimino

During the years we spent writing this book, a lot changed in Jessica's life. As we prepare for publication, she is twenty-seven years old and in a mature, joyful relationship with a man who respects her and provides stability and support. With him, she has found the ability to let her guard down, be vulnerable and trusting, and enjoy a healthy sexual relationship—all things she thought might never be possible for her. They are excited to be starting a family and building a future together. A few years ago, she freed herself from the box the abuse had confined her to, moving to her own apartment in Chicago and getting a job as a flight attendant. After years of being afraid to leave her grandparents' house or even her bedroom, she created a space of her own and embraced the opportunity to travel the world. She has since moved a couple more times, following the call of her heart to be closer to the family and friends who have supported her throughout her trauma and her transformation.

Jessica's growth is especially impressive considering how, meanwhile, so little has changed among the Tennessee community she transcended. Her stepfather was released from prison in 2020. Just as she expected, he was welcomed back into his family and his community. Jessica's mother and the church flock continue to deny his guilt and proclaim Jessica's—despite his conviction on thirteen counts, despite the eight years he spent in prison and the five denied appeals, despite his continued supervised probation and his lifelong violent sex offender status. They attempt to portray these as terrible things done to him rather than consequences of terrible things he did. They will likely cry out against what we've said in this book. They've already done so upon hearing we were working on it. They will continue to attempt to shame Jessica into silence and deny the difficult truths she had the courage to speak.

Just as Craig did throughout the trial, they will make a show of their criticisms as they cast the blame in the wrong direction. They will want you to pay no attention to the man behind the curtain.

But Jessica is moving on with her life. The actions of her estranged family and its blind supporters defined and constrained her for too many years. She is now carving out a future on her own terms, and she's come to recognize that that includes limiting who gets to be a part of it. After leaving a door cracked open for years in the hope that her mother might come knocking and make amends, she told me, "That door is now closed."

To me, it seems impossible to ignore the powerful perspectives of the several professionals who have so generously given their time and expertise in collaborating with us on this book and corroborating Jessica's story. Tommy and

Wayne, Laural, and Debbie have each worked with hundreds of victims and have in-depth knowledge of cases like these that most people could not stomach. Despite the numbers they have worked with and the years that have passed, they were all eager to help tell Jessica's story without hesitation. They remember her, they believe her, and they are appalled by how she was treated. In first introducing me to Jessica, Debbie told me that perhaps the most bizarre and troubling part of her past was what happened *after* the abuse.

As Laural explained it to me, in speaking out about what had happened to her, Jessica was a female child up against a powerful, wealthy, well-organized, "Christian," male-dominated base who supported white men they felt were lured into sin by their provocatively dressed female children. Laural acknowledged that it's very difficult to follow their logic, especially if you have not lived around this type of southern Christian. In the minds of many from that group who know Jessica's stepfather is guilty, yet continue to declare his innocence, what he did was not a sin, because he was not in control of his actions; rather, he was possessed by evil desires caused by Jessica.

Tommy was careful to make a distinction between this subgroup and the rest of the area's large Southern Baptist community. There are "a *lot*" of locals in the latter group, he told me, who have proven time after time to be highly charitable, to step up readily to help in emergencies and other difficult situations, assisting the police and other first responders in countless situations. "But that particular group," he delineated about Jessica's parents and their flock, "was not doing the Lord's work, I can tell you right now."

Wayne also described—early on, even directly to Jessica's mother, Melanie—the role he suspected Mitch's particular religion might be playing: perhaps his sense of morality prevented him from accusing Jessica of lying when he knew that what she was saying was true. Perhaps he couldn't bring himself to deny the allegations because doing so would require him to lie.

The hive mind of his supporters, meanwhile, readily cast blame and doubt not only upon Jessica but also upon Laural for prosecuting the case. She, too, dealt with the challenges of being a woman in a male-dominated atmosphere. Having prosecuted this case, throughout its various stages and multiple appeals, against several different all-male teams of attorneys, Laural summarized the attitude she was met with as: "I am a woman, and thereby weak." In the trial, Craig brought on another male attorney as co-counsel after "having difficulty" dealing with what the co-counsel described as Laural's "childish" nature, as quoted in one of the appellate courts' rulings. The year after Mitch was convicted, Laural was unceremoniously fired by the county, which she believes to be tied inextricably to her work on this case.

Laural is no weakling. She won more than ninety-five percent of the cases she took to trial. She was used to the odds being stacked against her: she had worked as her county's sole child support attorney at a time when there were eight thousand open cases; she later became the county's first specially designated child abuse prosecutor and its first female criminal prosecutor; and by the time she worked on Jessica's case some twelve years later, the county had grown to several times the size it was when she'd started, yet she remained its only prosecutor of child abuse and child rape cases. She told me that if she had not been the one to take on Jessica's case, "the whole situation would have been pushed under a rug with prayers and forgiveness for him, and admonishment and blame for Jessica. There would have been an even greater push to force her to accept guilt, repent, and ask her stepdad for forgiveness for tempting him."

The church flock funded many rounds of increasingly expensive attorneys to continue to appeal the guilty verdicts, desperate to replace the truth with the answer they wanted. "Many high-paid attorneys were hired to come up with the arguments and to blast Jessica and me," Laural told me. "But those arguments have been heard and considered by several appellate courts and found to have no merit."

Wayne and Tommy saw no merit in Mitch's arguments— or the lack thereof—from the night they first interviewed him at the police station. As Tommy put it, "We've talked to a lot of perps, and this guy did not answer one question correctly." When asked, for instance, if there's any truth to the allegations, saying "There shouldn't be" is not a good answer. Saying "It is what it is" is not a good answer. Tommy said Mitch's answers were "so bad," in fact, that there was no other choice but to arrest him. He had given them "every indicator of guilt." Letting detectives walk into your home to question your daughter without asking what's wrong and handing your car keys over at the police station, unasked, are not indications of innocence. "He knew," Wayne said of that behavior. "He knew what was coming."

It's important to remember that Wayne was initially among those who did not want to believe Mitch could be guilty. Wayne and his ex-wife had known the family for years. She was a coworker of Melanie's, was part of the same circle of church friends, and had often babysat Jessica and Caleb. Wayne's daughter had spent the night at Jessica's house. Wayne and Mitch had coached Little League football together, and Wayne had coached Caleb. When he first got the call the night of the report, Wayne had been so confident there was nothing to it that he wanted to go to make sure it was handled right. "There ain't no way," he recalled thinking. "I know this guy. Something's getting confused somewhere."

After asking Mitch just a couple of questions, though, Wayne's mind changed.

He felt he gave Mitch every out. "Tell me *something*," Wayne later described the conversation. "How 'bout telling me you didn't do it. How 'bout telling me she's a liar."

But Mitch could not do any of this.

Wayne lost sleep over the situation, going over and over it in his mind. Had there been any red flags in Jessica's story? Had Mitch said anything of substance that could clear the allegations?

Throughout her initial conversation with the detectives, Jessica's mother sounded not only nervous but highly defensive, irritated, like they were inconveniencing her. They described her demeanor as "a strong, angry denial," "looking for ways to blame everybody except the person that needs to be blamed." In this early stage, given the supposed shock of the news and the jet lag from her long trip home from Africa, they considered this behavior normal, and they told her as much. They understood that she was overwhelmed and that, of course, she would not *want* to believe this could be happening, that the entire subject was "too big" to process clearly.

But they did not expect that behavior to continue. As they watched the initial conversation at the station between Jessica and her mother, Tommy found it "concerning" that "there was no hug. There was no 'I love you.'" Rather, there was a ready line of questioning, "trying to trick her," as Wayne put it. He was concerned about the fact that, even before the abuse was reported, Jessica's mother's conversations with her were often like "interrogations"—a simple text message from a boy prompting, *Who is this? What are you doing?* Both detectives were struck by how quickly Melanie told them about lies Jessica told as a kid, seemingly looking to "tear down" her story now. When Tommy asked what other kinds of things Jessica would lie about, her mother rattled off vague examples like her grades, things that happened at school, or drama with her friends that her mother would sometimes have to get involved in to sort out. As Tommy told her, the distance between those kinds of lies and these allegations against Mitch is "one heck of a leap."

Tommy and Wayne estimate that they disproved about half of the cases that came to them. In such instances, the red flags would typically appear early on. These men have interviewed thousands of people. They are well versed in how liars operate, and that is not the behavior they saw in Jessica—not on the night they first interviewed her and not at any point throughout the four-year ordeal that followed. "I'd interviewed enough kids to know I was getting the truth," Tommy told me. A liar does not offer specifics like what she focused on to distract herself while the abuse was taking place or how the type of abuse would change when she had her period. The detectives emphasized to me how the core details of Jessica's story stayed the same over years, over so many hours of grilling—and that kids who lie can't keep that up. When backed into a corner, they'll most likely give up the act and tell the truth.

The detectives worried that that's precisely what Jessica's mother and her friends were trying to do: to beat Jessica down and antagonize her into changing her story, to take the easy way out. Or that Jessica would start to feel too badly about what this all would mean for Mitch and would say it didn't happen just to protect the family. Both men told me about the toll this kind of fight takes on victims; many cases fall through because the victim can't endure testifying in court and the long road it takes even to get there. Why would Jessica go through all of that over a lie? As Wayne put it, "Who loses their whole family because they got caught kissin'?"

Given his history with the family and their friend network, Wayne thought Melanie knew him well enough to know he wouldn't be making this up, that he wouldn't have arrested Mitch if he didn't feel he had to based on his interview. He thought she believed that he would not let Mitch go to prison—and that *Jessica* wouldn't let Mitch go to prison—because of a lie.

But things turned quickly.

The church flock rallied immediately, with no knowledge of the facts of the case, yet with plenty to say. They approached both Wayne and Tommy right away to question their involvement and their findings, and they were quick to ostracize Wayne's ex from their circle.

"What they should have said to Jessica's mother," Wayne told me, "was, 'We don't know what happened, and neither do you.'"

Debbie wondered if Melanie gained a sense of validation through the church group, who made her believe she was doing the right thing by not interacting with a child who had evil inside her. When thinking about the neglect this led to, Debbie told me, "Jessica was treated like a criminal."

From their earliest conversations—long before the enlarged Bible verse posters or holy water appeared—the detectives and DCS were concerned for Jessica's well-being, unsure that being at home with her mother was the best situation for her. "It hurt my teeth to watch them together," Tommy said.

He explained that this is why the guardian ad litem, Carol, was brought in to work on Jessica's behalf, to "get

Jessica some protection" after her mother and the defense team were "bringing in people from all over the place." Carol's involvement was supposed to prevent people from approaching Jessica about the case directly. Similarly, Tommy asked Melanie not to talk to Jessica about ramifications like Mitch going to prison or the family being broken apart. We've seen how little respect these directions received.

Tommy told Melanie directly that it gave him "an uneasy feeling" to have to send Jessica home with someone who was in frequent communication with the defense and was friends with the defense attorney's mother. "That's just spooky," he told her. "And it's improper." He had also gotten word of Melanie telling people at church, and at Mitch's bond hearing, and in a crowded elevator, that Jessica was a liar. "I cannot have Jessica in any situation where it's tampering with a state's witness. I just can't have it done," Tommy told Melanie in a recorded phone call. "And I will do whatever it takes to make sure that doesn't happen. I wanna make sure I'm *clear* on that."

It was the actions of the church group that led to BACA showing up to court in such awe-striking numbers. Laural told me that a few bikers had come to a different court date shortly before the appeal, which Jessica was not even aware of. There were maybe four or five of them, a much more typical presence in Laural's experiences in prior cases, and they sat down discreetly among the crowd of church supporters who filled the majority of the pews. The judge had ordered earlier that anyone who couldn't find a seat would have to wait out in the lobby. So, when the proceedings resumed after lunch that day, the church group made a point of spreading out to fill all of the available seating. The bikers had to climb over them to try to find spots to squeeze in. While working his way toward an empty space in the middle, around a row of feet of uncooperative people, one of the bikers tripped, nearly falling into the lap of a woman from the flock, who rushed off to the security guards' station with a mini flock of her own and tried to have the man arrested for assaulting her. In that one smaller appearance, then, BACA saw not only how poorly Jessica was being treated but how the shunning extended to anyone attempting to support her. The bikers put a call out online and quickly amassed the group of more than two hundred that came in for the appeal hearing. They came out to show Jessica she was supported *and* to show her antagonists that their actions have consequences.

"It's easy to see what they're doing," Wayne warned Aaron about the defense's camp in one of his initial interviews. "They're circling the wagons around Jessica to hope she'll break down. That's exactly what's happening here, and I don't care what anybody says. She has no support whatsoever."

Wayne and Tommy also warned Aaron that the defense would try to make Jessica seem like "a whore"—and that they were intentionally being crude in their conversations with him because of what he was sure to hear from the defense down the road. "I promise you, these are words you're going to hear," Wayne told Aaron. "They're gonna describe you and her as being the two worst people alive."

Aaron's story never changed, even when the detectives were the only other people in the room, even when they grilled him about how far he and Jessica had gone sexually, even when Tommy told him the rape kit could turn up Aaron's DNA if he had been in Jessica's "vaginal area" recently. The detectives pressed that now was the time to come clean if this was all a lie he and Jessica had concocted to get out of trouble for getting caught screwing around. And that they were going to be really mad if they found out later that they believed him when they shouldn't have.

He maintained throughout it all—including in court four years later—that they had only kissed, that they were not lying, and that he believed Jessica was telling the truth about what her stepdad had done to her.

Tommy and Wayne told Aaron that they believed her, too. And that defense teams tend to start picking apart peripheral stuff like this—like teenagers making out on a couch—when their case is weak.

The defense tried to make the prosecution's case seem weak because of the lack of physical evidence. In her first conversation with the detectives, Melanie wanted to know if the rape kit results had come back yet. While it's easy to understand the desire for something definitive in such a volatile situation, the detectives advised Melanie that those tests are often inconclusive, especially if the victim has gone to the bathroom or taken a shower, as Jessica had. They have even seen inconclusive test results in cases in which the assailant has confessed.

I spoke with one of the jurors from the trial, who acknowledged how frustrating the lack of evidence was in terms of how it limited the charges for which the jury was able to render a guilty verdict, how "unfair" it seemed that so much evidence was removed. I asked her if it was difficult to determine who was telling the truth, and she told me no, without hesitation. "I didn't doubt her for one second," she told me of Jessica. "I could just see the hurt and the pain in her little face. And the hurt and pain in her grandparents' faces. And the hurt and pain in her face when her mom went up there and her brother went up there." She said she couldn't imagine not believing her own child, and she scoffed at the trivial examples Melanie and the defense attempted to give to demonstrate Jessica's history as a liar. "Really? Are you serious? You call that lying?" she said to me in recounting her reaction. In fact, she said that argument was so flimsy that it was part of what convinced her Jessica was telling the truth.

The juror told me that the trial still haunts her. Prohibited from discussing it until after it was over, she said she would come home crying, or wake up in the middle of the night crying, and couldn't tell her husband what she was dealing with. She continued to have nightmares for months afterward. "My heart hurt so bad for this kid that felt so alone, that was not believed, that was shunned, that was degraded," she said. "That trial was the most traumatic thing I've ever experienced in my life—and I've experienced a lot of crazy things in my life."

While she still wishes their verdicts could have resulted in a longer prison sentence, she's grateful they were able to have Mitch put away for at least some bit of time, to give Jessica more of a window to try to heal, to know that that many more people believed her. "This kid deserved a chance to have a life," she said.

All of the experts involved in Jessica's story emphasized, not only to me but also throughout the investigation and trial, how important it is to help victims feel heard and believed, to tell them upfront that what happened to them is not their fault. "You've got to do whatever you can to help them feel safe," Debbie told me. That's why Nana was with Jessica for her first session with Debbie and was the one to give the details of what had happened. "Only after several months was Jessica able to talk about the abuse in general terms," Debbie said. "Often when she was asked specific questions about the abuse, she became silent and just stared." It took a long time and a lot of focused work for Jessica to push through her dissociative tendencies and start opening up to Debbie. That time and work were needed in order for her to trust, to feel safe.

Throughout my conversations with each of these experts, one phrase kept coming up, like a refrain: *I'd never seen anything like this.* As they recounted the family's and community's behavior, the church flock's presence permeating the courthouse, the dismissal of so much key evidence, and the further victimization of the victim throughout hours and weeks and *years* of court proceedings, they used words like *odd, nonsense, crazy, terrible, shocking, a blood bath, absolutely stunning*—and said that they'd never seen anything like this case. Imagine the things they have seen. And never anything like this.

They couldn't believe that the judges allowed Jessica to be questioned so incessantly, for so many hours, across the preliminary hearing, juvenile court, and the criminal trial, essentially allowing a whole trial at all three levels. There are systems in place that are supposed to prevent that, to protect the child, but the lack of assistance from Jessica's mother and the theatrics of the defense team complicated the entire process. Laural told me the reason she was not involved in the juvenile court hearing was that the defense argued that the temporary no-contact order DCS had issued was a separate matter from the criminal charges, and they requested that Laural be kept from that hearing in order to protect Mitch's rights against self-incrimination. Tommy and Carol were there but were ordered not to discuss the proceedings with Laural. So, everywhere they turned, it seemed, communication and information access were limited or outright denied. As Laural described it, the juvenile court hearing and the preparations for the trial "occurred simultaneously...but on totally different tracts even though they involved the same facts and the same players." And yet that juvenile court transcript was allowed to be reviewed and picked apart during the trial by the same defense attorneys who had asked the questions within it. Those attorneys "used this as a fishing expedition to isolate Jessica and to basically torment her into silence or submission," Laural told me. She and the detectives couldn't believe that entire interviews from the investigation were suppressed as evidence—not certain lines or snippets, but the entire conversations, dismissed. The detectives had never seen that happen in their decades-long careers. Nor had they ever seen the "non-offending parent" of a victim want an attorney.

"Let me put it this way," Tommy said to Melanie. "If the offender was not your husband, I guarantee you'd be up here every day talking to me, any time I wanted you to."

Typically, they would have expected the non-offending parent to cooperate with their investigation, to want to help, to want justice and closure.

But clearly, in so many ways, this was not a typical case.

"Child sex abuse crimes are incredibly serious for all involved," Laural emphasized to me. "No one wants to accuse a person of that type of crime without proof." But the limited access she and the detectives were granted to Jessica made it extraordinarily difficult either to confirm or to disprove the allegations. Still, they had best practices to follow and a thorough investigation to complete. So, like Jessica, they kept fighting forward. "We were not acting out of emotion or sympathy," Laural said. "Jessica was supported by us because her testimony, her demeanor, the evidence, and the circumstances led us to believe her and to believe her stepfather was guilty beyond a reasonable doubt."

"No matter who asks me, now or twenty years from now,

I'll say he's guilty," Wayne told me. "He had so many opportunities to deny it, and he didn't."

It couldn't have been easy, but despite the constant questioning and belittling hurled at Jessica's team by the rapist's
supporters, Wayne told me, "We weren't gonna take any guff
from any of them fools."

And Jessica and I won't either.

This is Jessica's truth. It is her story for the telling. I
applaud her for embracing the courage to tell it and am
honored that she allowed me to help her do so. In one of our
early meetings, she told me in a voice both exhausted by and
propelled by frustration, "Every time I tell my story, I apologize for my story."

She is done apologizing. The apology was never hers to
make.

Acknowledgments

From Jessica:

Working on this book over the last several years has helped me heal in more ways than one. I hope this book helps someone, even if it's in a small way. You are not alone, and you deserve the best life has to offer.

I will always be grateful for the hard work and dedication put into this book by Valerie Dimino. I am grateful for the patience you've shown me and your willingness to hear my story and help share it.

I am also grateful for my grandparents, Nana and Poppy, for helping me through one of the most difficult times in my life and always being there to love and support me. You've changed my life in more ways than you could imagine. I love you both all to pieces. Thank you for always picking me up when I was down.

To Bella, my best friend and companion, I will always love you.

To my amazing boyfriend who has provided so much support throughout this entire project, who always has an open mind and is willing to listen to me when I need someone to talk to.

To my son, I love you and always will.

To Wayne, Tommy, Laural, Sandy, and BACA for supporting and believing me throughout the entire process. I would not have gotten through it without your support and dedication.

To Debbie, for constantly working on the healing process with me and getting me to who I am today. I could not imagine where I would be if I didn't have your support.

To the victims and survivors of sexual assault, know you deserve to feel safe, you deserve to be believed, you deserve to tell your story whenever and to whoever you feel comfortable. You have a whole life ahead of you; this does not define you.

From Valerie:

I will forever be grateful to Jessica, Nana, and Poppy for entrusting me with this story, twice over: for your candor in sharing it with me as well as your generosity in being willing to share it with readers. And for answering my many questions, being patient with me as I learned, and revisiting deeply personal pain for the sake of a greater good. Jessica, your story matters, *you* matter, and you have profoundly affected my life and so many others' lives by speaking up.

I'm grateful also to Jessica's boyfriend for stepping up in the biggest ways in support of her and of this project. You made me feel welcome and trusted, and I knew immediately that I could welcome and trust you in return. Thank you.

My heart is brimming with thanks to so many people who were the puzzle pieces that turned this project from an abstract idea into a complete whole.

To Debbie for introducing me to Jessica and, in that moment, illuminating this entire path.

To Debbie, Tommy, Wayne, Laural, and Sandy for being there for Jessica at a time too few others were and being there again, all this time later, for both of us. Your expertise, perspectives, time, and tireless answering of my questions made an indescribable difference. And to the juror who spoke with me so openly and emotionally. Your perspective added such power, not just where you appear on the page but to my entire understanding of that courtroom battle. I thank you also for being there both then and now.

To the expert eyes who polished things up and made the process easy: Sarah Liu at Three Fates Editing, Carla Pinilla at Freaking Narnia, Clarissa Kezen at CK Book Cover Designs, and Amber Helt at Rooted in Writing.

To every single person who asked about the book, said they were eager to read it, encouraged me when I was feeling doubtful, and remained understanding as I pushed off plans and neglected messages while absorbed in this work, anxiety, and pandemic precautions. Throughout it all, you kept ushering me along. Especially to Jenny (my first and forever writing buddy), Kristi (my solopreneur inspiration), Cathy (my shifting-career-paths companion), Nicole, Kim, Anna, Megan A, Carla, Shea, Vicky, Megan L, Claire, Jess, Sara, Amanda, Ashley, Lauren, Sarah, Cherise, Warren, Allison, and Maria. I feel profoundly blessed to have so many dear friends to thank here.

To my Effervescent Writers group—Erika, Jess, Katie, and Camille—brought together by GrubStreet through some combination of chance and fate. You immediately felt like confidantes and soulmate sisters. Our monthly check-ins are the most beautiful combination of inspiration, friendship, and therapy.

To Angie and my other fantastic colleagues for being so supportive about this project and about my working part time, and to April for being not only a fantastic colleague but an equally fantastic publishing guru.

To my professors at SUNY Brockport, who helped me

discover the writer I am and the writer I want to be, many of whom read various drafts of this work or met with me about its potential. Especially to Anne Panning, whose generous guidance warmed and reassured my anxious heart, and to Steve Fellner, for letting me talk him into a summer independent study, as well as to Jim Whorton, Ralph Black, Greg Garvey, Meg Norcia, and MJ Iuppa. And to Sarah Freligh, who is such a mentor she feels like an honorary professor and who shared a pivotal lunch chat with me in a 90-degree café.

To the other writers giving voice to these difficult truths that so desperately need to be heard, especially to Chessy Prout and Jenn Abelson, Lacy Crawford, Michelle Bowdler, and Chanel Miller, whose astounding memoirs served as torches lighting the way.

To Leah, forever and ever.

To my amazing family, especially to my parents for not trying to talk me out of being an English major, to Dad for the nudge toward marketing, and to Mom for reading multiple drafts and talking through endless hours of questions, what-ifs, fears, and doubts and turning them into possibilities. To Russ and Josh for being wonderful friends in addition to wonderful brothers; to Amanda and Jackie for being the kindest and most fabulously fun sisters-in-law; and to Dominic, Landon, Cora, and Eden, who won't be old enough to read the rest of this book for some years yet but who I hope always know how much love and joy they add to my life.

To Rich, who believed in the writer in me before I did, enough to build her a backyard writer's cabin; who continues to respond to my wishes to be a writer by saying, "You *are* a writer"; and who helped me build myself back up and start discovering my best self. I'm grateful every day for you.

And to each and every reader, for helping me realize this dream I've had since my earliest memories.

To learn more about Bikers Against Child Abuse (BACA) or donate to their life-changing work, please visit bacaworld.org.

About the Authors

Jessica Renee is no longer defined by the trauma that altered her childhood. It is one building block of who she has become: a strong advocate for herself and others, a loyal friend and grateful granddaughter, a cozy homemaker, a devoted partner, and a mom to a wonderful son and two mischievous cats.

 **Valerie Dimino** has been passionate about writing since kindergarten, when her first short story—written and illustrated in marker—was graced with an "I'm Proud of You!" dinosaur stamp. She earned bachelor's and master's degrees in creative writing from SUNY Brockport and has 14 years of professional writing, editing, and marketing experience in higher education, performing arts, and medical informatics. She lives in Lakeville, New York, with her partner, Rich. This is her first book.

valeriedimino.com

  @valeriedimino